O Sane and Sacred Death

"It is good to find someone who will explore the process of dying and what lies beyond death in as simple and comfortable a way as Louise Ireland-Frey has done in this book. It brings an event often dripping in mystery and dread into full and candid view. Here death can finally be understood to be a simple and often joyous transition."

—Winafred Lucas, Ph.D., author of
Regression Therapy: A Handbook for Professionals

"Louise Ireland-Frey is perhaps the most gentle soul I have met in my entire life's journey. Yet with an inspiring courage, she steps directly into the midst of such highly controversial milieus as spirit possession and after-death survival. What she writes rings true for me; I have personally experienced much of what she describes. She has made a grand contribution to our knowledge of the spiritual reality."

—William J. Baldwin, Ph.D., author of
Spirit Releasement Therapy: A Technique Manual

"This well-written, well-documented, and easy-to-read book is a beautiful resource for the reader and brings light and understanding."

—Gladys Taylor McGarey, M.D., M.D.(H)

"This important work continues the pioneering efforts of Edgar Cayce and Edith Fiore. Louise Ireland-Frey, M.D., is a respected therapist; we scientists can continue to stretch our traditional boundaries."

—Logan H. Roots, M.D.

"*O Sane and Sacred Death* by Louise Ireland-Frey, M.D., is a spiritual view of death and of the afterlife. It includes many interesting case histories of people who have had Near-Death Experiences, as well as explorations of deaths remembered during hypnosis. Her book has wonderful and inspiring stories to tell of various types of death, what happens to animals after death, how family members can be comforted, communications with those who have died, and what life is like in after-death realms. Dr. Ireland-Frey has done a thorough study of many aspects about dying, and gives us so many examples in each area that make her book a valuable addition to the field of the study of death. This is a book that you will want to read all at once, it's so fascinating!"

—Rabia Clark, Ph.D., Certified Past Life Therapist
and Hypnotherapist, author of
Past Life Therapy, the State of the Art

"*O Sane and Sacred Death* by Louise Ireland-Frey, M.D., is a welcome addition to the growing body of evidence related to the existence of consciousness beyond the physical body. Dr. Ireland-Frey shares her vast personal experiences related to the subject of death, as well as her broad professional experiences as an M.D. and a hypnotherapist. . . . I recommend *O Sane and Sacred Death* to anyone who is dealing with this issue in their personal lives, as well as to those who wish to expand their knowledge of current consciousness research."

—Janet Cunningham, Ph.D., President, International
Assoc. for Regression Research and Therapies

O SANE AND SACRED DEATH

FIRST PERSON ACCOUNTS OF DEATH

AS RECEIVED IN HYPNOTIC REGRESSIONS

LOUISE IRELAND-FREY, M.D.
Certified Clinical Hypnotherapist

Blue Dolphin

Published by Blue Dolphin Publishing, Inc.
P.O. Box 8, Nevada City, CA 95959
Orders: 1-800-643-0765
Web: www.bluedolphinpublishing.com

ISBN: 1-57733-090-0

Library of Congress Cataloging-in-Publication Data

Ireland-Frey, Louise.
    O sane and sacred death : first person accounts of death (as
    received in hypnotic regressions) / Louise Ireland-Frey.
        p. cm.
    Includes bibliographical references.
    ISBN 1-57733-090-0
        1. Death—Miscellanea. 2. Reincarnation. I. Title.

    BF 1442.D43 174 2001
    133.9′01′3—dc21

                                                    00-068045

Printed in the United States of America

10   9   8   7   6   5   4   3   2   1

To all who will die
now, soon, or much later,
this book is joyously dedicated.

... fresh as the morning, thus would I chant a song for you,
    O sane and sacred death. . . .

And I knew death, its thought, and the sacred knowledge of
    death.

Then with the knowledge of death as walking one side of me,
And the thought of death close-walking the other side of me,
And I in the middle as with companions, and as holding
    the hands of companions,
I fled forth to the hiding receiving night that talks not, . . .
And the voice of my spirit tallied the song of the bird.

Come lovely and soothing death,
Undulate round the world, serenely arriving, arriving,
In the day, in the night, to all, to each,
Sooner or later delicate death. . . .

Dark mother always gliding near with soft feet,
Have none chanted for thee a chant of fullest welcome?
Then I chant it for thee, I glorify thee above all,
I bring thee a song that when thou must indeed come,
        come unfalteringly.

Approach, strong deliveress,
When it is so, when thou has taken them I joyously sing the dead,
Lost in the loving floating ocean of thee,
Laved in the flood of thy bliss, 0 death.

        Walt Whitman, "When Lilacs Last in the Dooryard Bloomed"

CONTENTS

FOREWORD

As a young physician in a small Ohio river town with a growing family of four small children, I found myself one day face to face with my eldest son who was seven years old. His big brown eyes were filled with tears as he said to me, "Mama, why did you let Tommy die? Why did you let him die?" My only answer to him at that time was, "Carl, I did all I could. There wasn't anything more I could do." Then I held him, and the two of us cried together.

Forty-five years later that scene is still etched in my mind. Tommy had been Carl's best friend. He had developed appendicitis, which had ruptured, and in spite of everything that the surgeon, the pediatrician, and I could do, little Tommy had died.

My son is now an orthopedic surgeon and since experiencing the death of a patient is part of the life of a physician, he has had to face similar situations. Unfortunately, in our culture we have equated the death of a patient as a failure on our part. As if we were some sort of deity and could "save" every patient that we worked with, and that death would not be part of our experience.

I remember a wonderful, elderly patient of mine who was 104 years old. When I said to him, "How you doing, Harry?" He said, "Just fine. My parents take care of me." I said, "What do you mean 'parents'?" He said, "Father time,

Mother nature." I have always cherished his beautiful response, and when his time to make the transition came, he did it very gently and peacefully in his sleep.

The longer I practice medicine the more aware I become of the reality that the number of days that we spend on this earth are not as important as the quality of life with which we live each day. Little Tommy lived only seven years but affected my life and the life of my son throughout all these years.

It's truly wonderful if we can live to a "ripe old age," especially if our primary purpose is not just to live to be old. Jesus didn't say, "I came to give you long life." He said "I came to give you life and that more abundantly."

The more we understand about life and death and really comprehend that death is not our enemy, the more we can live an abundant life.

Louise Ireland-Frey's extremely well-documented, scientifically validated book is also highly readable and thoroughly interesting. She gives us material to work with in our continuing search for an "abundant life," with all its dimensions and relationships.

Gladys Taylor McGarey, M.D., M.D. (H),
Scottsdale Holistic Medical Group

Preface

When I was a young doctor in Wichita, Kansas, in 1942, a lady came to my office, her eyes strained with fear.

"Just recently while I was walking in the garden with my father, he dropped dead with a heart attack, and a few years ago my uncle died that way, just dropped dead. I'm so afraid that I am going to die anytime the way they did."

I looked at her a moment and decided to take the chance of shocking her into a calmer attitude. "Yes," I agreed quietly, "I think you will die."

She stared, speechless.

"I am going to die, too," I went on, "and I may die before you do. Tomorrow morning I may get hit by a car as I cross the street to my office here. The main difference between us is that you think you know how you are going to die, and I do not know how I may die."

She was still staring; but I could see that she was listening.

"And what if we do die? It's like shedding an overcoat, that's all." I drew a piece of paper to me and began to write. "There is first your physical body; then you have your feelings and emotional system, which I call the astral body; and you have the mind or mental body with its thoughts and ideas; and then you have the soul or the part that goes on evolving. Beyond these is your spirit, the spark of the divine.

"Now, when your father died, he lost his body." I crossed out the words *physical body* on the sheet of paper. "That is the only thing your father lost. All these others, his feelings, his mind, his soul, his spirit, he still has. And so will you when you die."

We talked a little while longer. I examined her, listened carefully to her heart, and sent her for an electrocardiogram. She was calmer when she left.

A few days later the report on the cardiogram came back, "Borderline." I phoned to tell her of the report and advised, "Just try to live sensibly."

Several weeks later I saw her in the pharmacy. I asked the usual question, "How are you?"

"Disgustingly healthy!" she answered with a wide smile.

With that healthy attitude I felt that her heart would probably continue to tick steadily for a good long time!

This was in 1942. The war had begun for us after Pearl Harbor, and my husband, like most other young male doctors, had gone into the Service. I was attempting to carry on his medical practice—which he had inherited only a few months previously from a doctor who had entered the Navy. My health was not good. I fought fatigue constantly, and weakness increased until at last I knew that my prediction to my cardiac patient about the manner of my possible death might well become reality—either in my car or as a pedestrian—were I to become too vague to notice an oncoming car or too weak to avoid it. Reluctantly and yet with vast relief I closed the practice in 1943 and went to live with my parents in Colorado.

The war finally ended. My husband returned and we chose western Colorado for our home. Our plans for a family, long delayed, came into being with four sons born between 1948 and 1954. While my husband took up the medical practice of a former doctor, I stayed at home and tried to adjust to domestic life. It was not easy. Small children require constant care, patience, teaching, supervision, and much love, and I had very little strength or energy for their physical or emotional needs. I simply did the best I could, and that often was not very good at all.

In 1955 while I was still struggling with motherhood and continuing weakness (now called Chronic Fatigue Syndrome), a couple of friends from California taught me techniques by which to contact so-called "Cellular Consciousness," and with one of them and a few other friends I experimented with hypnosis and regression-work during 1956 and 1957 for several hundred hours, all told. This was mostly just for fun and curiosity rather than therapy.

In 1971 my husband and I were divorced after thirty-two years of marriage. The youngest son left for college the next year. Slowly I began to get back into the medical field by accepting the care of patients in a nursing home.

Late in 1978 a nurse-friend insisted on my taking a self-hypnosis course. "It helped me so much that I'm sure it will help you," she urged. It was sixteen hours of lecture and workshop and included the psychology of the subconscious mind, some techniques for self-regression, and even a simple method for contacting the power of Universal Mind to help *others* through one's *self*-hypnosis. This course, taught by Richard E. Margis, an instructor of the American Council of Hypnotist Examiners, gave me at last the tool I needed, and my health began to improve steadily as I talked to my subconscious mind.

During the following year, 1979, I took many more hours of professional training in hypnosis, plus the input of workshops, seminars, and books, and became a certified hypnotherapist, starting a new and most satisfying career at age sixty-seven.

The next year, 1980, I enrolled with three friends in a series of six-week courses in Extra-Sensory Perception, taught by a young woman, Nan Taylor, who had spent twenty years in the study and whose psychic talents were highly developed. These courses, totalling seventy-two hours, fit in very well with the hypnotic techniques I had learned and increased the perceived possibilities of hypnosis. I admit that through all the ESP courses I was full of doubts and questions! The proof that I had found for self-hypnosis was in my renewed health and energy. So, in the ESP classes I tried to keep an open mind, waiting for "proofs."

It was in these classes that the other students and I became acquainted with spiritual advisors. In 1980 I had the first "reading" of my life from a psychic. Nan sat facing me and let herself go into an altered state, and then permitted another consciousness to use her vocal apparatus.

Thus it was that I first met a disembodied intelligent entity who conversed with me. He was Demetrius, wise, patient, firm—and free with suggestions while insisting that I had my own decisions to make. He impressed all of us students. Demetrius helped the instructor as she taught us; he was our teacher as much as she was. Nan told us that, disillusioned in her previous discarnate advisor, she had asked that a "master" come to channel through her, and we students all agreed that Demetrius was truly a master.

In one of the classes we asked to "see" our spiritual advisors. Nan told us that they were only temporary masters for each of us. As we sat in silent openness, meditating with closed eyes, one of the students saw, as my temporary master, a Germanic man. Another saw a Chinese face behind my shoulder. I did not see anything or anyone; I *felt* or *heard,* or recognized *thoughts* that came into my mind.

Wilhelm, a German poet, apparently specialized in pupils who were in some sort of transition, as I was, selling my beloved but decrepit old home and looking for a new place. Over the next months I became rather well acquainted with his Puckish sense of humor and his quiet teasing. Before he left me I had found a suitable house. He signaled me with a longer-than-usual flute-tone in my ear, and I felt his thought, "Now you can go ahead on your own," with a subtle emphasis on CAN. I felt that it meant he trusted my ability to go ahead into the future without his help.

And the Chinese doctor—whom ten or twelve friends have seen, although I have not—is described by all of them in the same way, though only four of these people know each other. He accepts the nickname "Master Ching," a name that one of the women in the meditation group playfully applied to him because his gentle wisdom reminded her of the *I Ching* quotations of the Kung Fu master in the television series by that name. I know now that he is not just a temporary master.

For a long time "Master Ching" withheld his personality. Channeled through different friends at one time or another, he always spoke in few cogent words, usually answering a question with another question and emphasizing free will in all matters. More recently he has expanded his channels to include more of my friends. Of course he may have dozens or hundreds of pupils in other locales, some of whom he may speak through.

He himself has been changing toward us, allowing himself more expressions of humor, more direct but gentle admonitions, more urgent suggestions about our activities and our time schedules, and of late even allowing us glimpses of his personal life in the Chinese incarnation: He said he was fond of my young weeping willow. He likes willow trees— they hung over the river where he used to enjoy fishing. And he knows about my dear old cat, the latest in a long series of pets we have had. Master Ching occasionally mentions Smokey with smiling affection: "Your cat will like that."

In 1983 Vickie Mongrain, a psychically talented young friend, was doing research with me on death and the conditions after death, using hypnosis as our means of contacting such information. We intended to write a book together. Then we were told by her spiritual advisor that more data needed to be accumulated before the actual writing should be started. I had numerous other duties and activities to distract me, and the forty-mile round trip for her to come to my home was not always convenient for her, and so the work languished. Not long after we had begun really solid work, she and her family moved to another town. The valuable material that we did obtain, however, is included in the present book. I am very grateful for her generous expenditure of time and gasoline back then, for her enthusiasm and remarkable channeling, and also for the assistance of her spiritual advisor, "White Hair of Wisdom," who asked us to call him "Grand Father."

Before my work with Vickie and since then, I have continued to have experiences with death: my mother, my father, and many relatives and close friends have died. I have had regressions to a dozen or so of my own deaths in previous lives. I have been a hypnotherapist for a good many hundred clients over the past twenty years—plus a few scattered ones since 1957—who have re-experienced their deaths in a past life or have felt another soul's death-experience during "releasement therapy." (*Releasement* is the contact with, conversation with, and release of a disembodied soul living in the client's body or in someone else's body.)

Now it is the time in my life for "fruit gathering," as the poet Tagore would call it. This book—at the urging and with the encouragement of Master Ching and my dear friends— is one of the autumnal fruits that I offer now.

ACKNOWLEDGMENTS

THESE ARE THE STORIES of many patients, clients, friends, and co-workers in addition to my own. Most of them have given permission for me to mention them by name. In those few instances when I felt it appropriate, I have used a false name, enclosing it the first time in quotation marks.

My thanks go to each one.

To Vickie Mongrain, with whom I first began research on death, go special thanks, and also to the friends who contributed written examples of their encounters, direct or indirect, with death: Psychic Carroll Armstrong, Dr. Hazel Denning, Social Worker Bernice Garber, Hypnotherapist Karen Russell Roots, and Nurse Charlene Smith.

Deep gratitude also goes to the friends, students, and co-workers who have done so much remarkable channeling: Nurse Lanetta Carson, Artist Mary Farmer, Artist Kathleen Hawkins, an exceptional student L.B., and also Nurse V.Y. It is hard to know where to end the list!

The authors from whose letters or articles I have selected references I sincerely appreciate, as well: Dr. William Baldwin, Captain Jacques-Yves Cousteau, Minette Crowe, Lord Hugh Dowding, Dr. David V. Lee, and Dr. David Lorimer. I thank all these for allowing me to quote or reprint excerpts from their writings. The origin of each reference has been noted in the text.

And of course to the dozens of patients, students, and friends, both named and unnamed, whose stories are included here, I offer not only my appreciation but also my warm feelings of deep connection. In our sessions we lived and died together.

Not least do I thank the Chinese doctor whom we playfully but respectfully call Master Ching. It is he who, with Dr. Susan McGinness, has fostered, critiqued, suggested, and encouraged the development of this book at each stage of the writing. The fact that I now live and work in Durango is due to Master Ching's suggestion and the tremendous help from Susan and the other members of our meditation group: Ann Jacobs, R.N.; Harry Rosenberg, A.B.D.; Cynthia Sharp, A.B.D.; also Reece Kelly, Ph.D., and others. They made the move easy for me and continue to assist in all possible ways in the works assigned to me, especially Susan with her page-by-page suggestions.

Anita Hermosillo typed the final draft of the book not only with her fingers but with her heart, feeling that she was directed to work on this particular writing because of the death of one very close to her only a year ago. She has thanked me just as I thank her for her careful assistance.

I

INTRODUCTION

Why "First Person"?

DYING AND DEATH are almost always peaceful. It is beforehand that there is pain, fear, and struggle. Nurses report the almost universal quietude and ease with which their terminal patients slip away. Theirs are first-hand reports of what they see and hear as their patients complete the life cycle.

This book goes one step farther, reporting what the patients themselves (sic) tell us after their bodies have died; in other words, these are *first person reports of dying and death*: "I died . . . I knew I was dead. . . ." I have compiled several different classes of these first-person reports.

First of all are *my own.* I have contacted about sixteen previous lives and have passed through the death experience ending several of those lives. I can say, "Yes, I have died before and I know what it is like to die." Of course each death is different from all others, yet all have similarities.

Second are my *clients' past-life deaths* as experienced during hypnotic sessions. These are told to me in first person: "I floated up . . . I could look down and see my body. . . ."

Third are the death-experiences of souls I have "released" from my clients. Not being part of the client's own self or psyche as multiple personalities are, each obsessing soul (see Glossary) has its own life history and death history.

1

I have released hundreds of such *obsessing souls* from my clients by *"Releasement"* techniques (see Glossary), and their death stories make as large a group as those of clients' past-life deaths.

Fourth are the death-experiences of various types of *"earth-bound souls"* contacted and assisted *("Rescued")* through the channeling of psychic friends or persons in hypnosis, e.g., wandering souls, ghosts, poltergeists, and so on, including most suicides. All of these are souls in need of help. After assisting a group of suicides to pass from their state of despair into a higher state, the person who was the channel told us, "Their feelings of gratitude were almost overwhelming." (Incident at a workshop which the channel, Mary L. Farmer, and I gave in 1992.)

For me and many other therapists the thought of "death in the first person" is quite ordinary. Thousands of people have had spontaneous flash-backs to a past life; tens of thousands have had a regression to a past life by a therapist or facilitator. Edith Fiore and Dick Sutphen alone have re-gressed thousands, and the list of other fine therapists who also perform past-life regressions is too long to add here. And *if we have lived before, we have died before.*

Death is only a transition. Not only do I "believe" that but I feel that I know it. The psyche, the consciousness, persists past the death of the physical body. The death experience is to be accepted as simply as the birth experience, and both are included in the meaning of Life. Laws and religions, cultures and mores, have nothing to do with the physiology of the birth processes or death processes and do no more than color the psycho-spiritual changes occurring for the psyche, the soul.

How one lived, how one died, the pervading thoughts, emotions, and unfinished business at the time of death all seem to provide some of the core issues that set up the lessons in the next lives. I became aware through my clients' reliving of their past lives that the vows, the intense desires, fears, loves, and other emotions, and the habitual mental patterns are controlling factors lifetime after lifetime, fully as important as the physical events and traumata of those lives or the present lifetime.

All this implies a "belief" in *reincarnation*. Yes, but I agree with modern researchers (Jane Roberts, Dick Sutphen, and others) who emphasize that the journey of a soul is not a simple linear movement from past through present into future, with exact repayment of "bad" karma or "good" karma to the person responsible for creating that karma. There is more complexity to the journey of a soul than simplistic straight-line reincarnation. For the present book, however, it seems advisable to accept temporarily this simpler concept, which is easier to understand and does have much worthwhile value for each of us in our growing toward a spiritual life.

In the journey of the soul, rebirth occurs again and again, and death occurs again and again. A minister who had studied ancient writings told me that one translation of Jesus' answer in John 3:3, in which Nicodemus asked the great Teacher a question, is "Except a man be *born again and again,* he cannot see the kingdom of heaven." Jesus accepted the concept of reincarnation when he reminded his disciples that Elijah (Elias) had indeed come before him, as prophesied, but that men had taken Elijah and had done with him "as they listed." "Then the disciples understood that he was speaking to them of John the Baptist" (Matthew 17:13). Yet John, you may recall, had denied that he was Elijah. Memory of past lives is totally obliterated for most of us. So we are left to choose whom to believe, John or Jesus. John's father, before John's conception, had been told by Gabriel that he would have a son who "will go . . . in the spirit and power of Elijah" (Luke 1:17).

At another time the Teacher was questioned by his disciples about a certain blind man: "Who did sin, this man or his parents, that he was *born blind?*" Were they asking whether the blind man had sinned while a babe in the womb? How could a fetus sin so terribly? Or did they mean the man's former self in a previous lifetime must have sinned and was now reaping the just recompense? Or had his parents deserved to be burdened with a blind child for *their* sins? The reply of the Teacher was brief and succinct: "Neither did this man sin nor his parents that he was born blind,[1] but that the works of God should be made manifest in him."

Well, wait a minute! Does that mean that a just, merciful God afflicted an innocent person with total blindness just to give publicity to the powers this same God had given to another Son, the Teacher? Or does it mean that, in accordance with the law of free will, the man's Soul (Higher Self) had *volunteered* to be born blind in order to become, eventually, a clear and undeniable example of the powers of the Master for helping the unhelpable, for curing the incurable?

Until a number of my own clients began presenting me with similar cases of such selfless decisions made by the Soul before birth (or even before conception), I thought Jesus' explanation showed a cold-hearted attitude on the part of the man's Soul, if not indeed on the part of the Creator! It does seem to me that sometimes the Higher Self, the Soul, may make such a decision without comprehending just how hard the experience chosen may turn out to be when the entire consciousness is confined to the lower self in the

---

[1] Those interested may wish to refer to the tape of a 1983 lecture, "Regressing the Blind to their Former Lives," by Dr. Jim Pareke and Paul Palmer, an account of their personal research. Address 8751 Osborne, Highland, TN 46322; Phone (218) 838-2770.

dense, heavy, earth-plane with its attendant miseries and loneliness.

Have we all had previous lives? The answer seems to be, "Yes, and probably many of them." Why do we not remember them? Many people do not even remember early childhood experiences or the birth experience, so why expect to recall consciously a past life? Many people do remember a past life, however, especially in childhood. Children may comment to the mother something like, "When I was big and you were little . . ." (as quoted by Joanne DiMaggio, in the *APRT Newsletter*, Vol. 14, No. 3 Summer, 1994).

Two fathers, living hundreds of miles apart, both wrote me telling of the prattlings of their four-year-old children about what seemed to be past lives; their letters came to me only weeks apart. I sent each parent the address of the other, so each would feel less alone and confused. Most parents, regrettably, are usually too busy to listen to a small child's chatter. "She has a large imagination," the parents say indulgently, or even, "He is quite a little liar at times." This perhaps common tendency of children to remember past lives seems to evaporate at about the age of five or six, in most cases.

Some older people have occasional flash-backs to a past life, or at least to circumstances that are not those of the present life. A neighbor of mine told me that she woke one morning feeling a motion unlike any that she had ever felt before—and then she began to see a desert scene, and found herself riding on a camel! And I, though born and raised in inland states, had several flash-backs at about the age of eleven or twelve to a time when I was a young boy living in a hut on top of a cliff that faced an ocean on the east: Maine, I wondered, or China? China, I felt.

If a person has had no such flash-backs and has never had a regression to a past life through the assistance of a therapist, it is understandable that he or she will have doubts: "How do you know that it is your life you are contacting? Why not someone else's life? Or are you just making it all up?"

When a person himself has contacted a past-life experience, however, there remains little doubt because the emotions, the physical sensations, and the small details are vivid and realistic. So it is with me. I have gone through the death experience more than once.

The first time for me was a repeated flash-back, in full consciousness, of dying as the Chinese boy who had carelessly let himself be caught in his favorite cove by the incoming tide. I felt myself as the little boy being tugged farther and farther toward the deep water as I struggled to swim to a safer place. Being a good swimmer, I believed I could make it. When I realized that I could not, I turned my energies to trying to swim to a pile of rocks near the middle of the cove, where I hoped the waves would dash me gently and I could stand on the rocks, nearly submerged, until the tide went out again. But the waves were not gentle. I could not break their force as they hurled me onto the stones. I died with the clear perception that my death was due to my own carelessness; I was filled with regret. I thought of my gentle fisherman father, who had often sternly ordered me not to play in that cove while he was absent. I had disobeyed him, and now I was dying, and he would grieve; he would be sad and very lonely.

The second time I remembered dying (Doesn't that sound interesting?) was many years later in 1954 when a friend regressed me into a past life and I found myself a young woman dying after an extremely hard childbirth. The stillborn baby, after dying in utero, had to be removed in sections. Worn out by the ordeal, I lay passively, barely conscious. A nun with whom I had become friends visited me and said softly, "I heard you were ill, dear, so I brought you these," and she placed her rosary in my hand. Although I was not Catholic, I appreciated her gift, knowing that she had little of her own to offer. I smiled without words, she kissed my cheek and left. I closed my eyes and presently felt the rosary falling slowly from my fingers. It was hard to breathe, yet my body longed for oxygen. The conflict continued until, at long last, *I got that breath!* (My facilitator friend told me afterward that she was afraid I was actually dying right there before her eyes, except that she could see a pulse in my neck that seemed to be steady. *She* was greatly relieved when I took that deep breath!)

That breath was the last one I took in that lifetime. It relieved the anoxia and allowed me to relax. I drifted up and began to feel a little thrill of anticipation. But my body seemed to be hanging onto my feet. I wanted to kick it off, thinking, "The poor old thing." Then somehow I did get rid of it, and I peacefully floated on higher in a mood of quietness and yet eagerness, like, "What now?" (This was the end of that experience.)

After I became a hypnotherapist professionally, people began coming to me as a last resort, either because previous therapy and self-examination had revealed no good reason for their current problems or life patterns or merely because they had questions, such as, "Why me?" or, "What am I supposed to be doing in this world?" The altered state of consciousness has enabled clients to discover hidden emotional or spiritual causes that have explained certain life difficulties or have shed light on their questions. This schema involving reincarnation, karma, and individual soul-evolvement has become the basis for my constantly broadening therapeutic work. It has been the needs or questions of clients that have kept pushing me into more and more corners of the psychospiritual world! Many is the time when I have felt, in total bewilderment, "Now what do I do? What in the world can I do to help this person or to answer this person's question?" My attempts to help, however, have been extremely educational. They have required courage and my willingness to go along with whatever the client is receiving, and to wade right into deep waters, foregoing judgments on the mental level until later.

Method

The method I have used since the mid-fifties is the simple one I still use, although with refinements and additions learned through the years as well as various short-cuts and a much more clearly marked spiritual orientation.

After greeting a new client and getting a few minutes of basic information, including whether she has ever meditated, regularly or not (for meditation "gives a head start on hypnosis," I explain), I discuss the client's problem or questions, describe hypnosis, and mention the fact that *the person in hypnosis is still aware on the conscious level and is in control* of her own reactions. Sometimes I offer a two- or three-minute demonstration of hypnotizing her, "just as you sit there." If the client says she is ready to "go right to work," however, I use a quiet, brief induction with the client lying comfortably on a cot or a recliner chair and deepen the altered state to a medium depth.

For the first session I use, as deepening, a guided meditation or visual imagery which includes many suggestions of a therapeutic nature, recognizable by the client's subconscious mind even if not by her conscious mind as she rests *in hypnosis, conscious and aware* of every word that is being spoken. Such a suggestion may be frankly expressed as being symbolic: "The little hill is a symbol for your will-power, patience, resolution—all of these just as firm and dependable as the solid little hill," and so on.

Next I follow with a clearing technique, using symbols again which the client's subconscious mind understands and accepts calmly as reality—for instance, that a soft whisk broom is brushing out such things as anger, fear, guilt, grief, and their causes. Since the causes of these emotions may be lying deep in the subconsciousness and it is in this altered state (hypnosis) that the client's subconscious mind is listening alertly to every suggestion, it is easy for the subconscious mind to follow directions in a very literal way. Not all of these negative emotions can be eradicated by this method, of course, but a surprising amount of good can be accomplished.

Next, the "spaces" created by the elimination of the negative things need to be filled with positives such as courage, strength, wisdom, self-confidence. I offer all of these either verbally by the simple words or by visualizations and symbols.

I also routinely program that one of the client's fingers is a *"Yes" finger* and another as a *"No" finger*, telling the subconscious mind to answer questions by causing the appropriate finger to twitch or lift up. This is called using *Ideomotor Finger Movements*.

Now the client is ready for whatever her *subconscious* mind feels is important for her to work on. Usually I simply ask the subconscious mind to select whatever is the basic cause of the problem, or the event that is the one we are "supposed" to get today. This wording indicates that either the subconscious mind of the client or her Higher Mind knows better than I what is important—in fact, better than her own conscious mind. For instance, one elderly lady believed that her painful shoulder was what she needed to have worked on, but her subconscious mind took us to a long-forgotten childhood incident. When the pain, fear, and other trauma of the childhood incident were cleared hypnotically, her shoulder automatically seemed to be freed of pain and limitation and after this one session became increasingly useful.

Such going back to an earlier event is called *Regression* and is an accepted and widely used technique of very many hypnotherapists. Instead of going back to an event in the client's childhood, the subconscious mind may take the client's awareness back farther, to the birth experience, or to intrauterine times, or to a past life. The wording of the therapist can direct which of these is to be received, but when given *carte blanche,* the subconscious mind will bring up whatever it deems of greatest importance to have the client contact.

An example of the subconscious mind's wisdom is the session of a young woman who came to me because of her great fear of death. Without directing her subconscious mind to go to any specific time or event, I simply used the open-ended instruction, "Let your mind take us to *whatever is most valuable for you to get today.*"

In hypnosis she found herself as a small girl alone near some primitive grass huts. The sun was extremely hot and she wanted to gain shelter in one of the huts, but she knew that dead people were in them and she feared to go in, lest the spirits of the dead would "get" her. In spite of the terrible heat and the flies, she remained outside, alone and frightened.

I asked her to go back in time and see why she was here. She found, with tears, that her tribe had deliberately "lost" her.

"There's a big gathering—too many people, and I'm a girl. There's not enough to eat. It's been dry, hot . . . everything is dry and it's . . . I think they are all going to leave. I don't want to be left to die. I know they are going to do that—they think I don't know, but I know; I can see it in their eyes, the shutting out.... It's not my family that takes me—it's somebody else; it's his job. My family's eyes are sad—not *his* eyes . . . I'm the youngest. . . .

"They're all leaving, and I stay by the houses. The man took me by the houses where people have already died—a lot of empty houses. . . . I want to say, 'No! No!' but you don't tell him 'No.' I don't open my mouth.

"I can hardly move—the flies are terrible—my mouth is so dry. I'm sick, too. That's why they left me . . . I get weaker—weaker—it's so dark . . . dizziness . . . then sleep.

"That's all . . . It's not so bad . . . The pain's gone, the pain in my head and stomach. . . . I see my body down there. Flies all over. . . The dizziness is better, just like floating, flying; nothing hurts. Feels good. I can't feel afraid now. It feels so good not to care, not to hurt any more.

". . . I'm going now. I like it, just going into the night . . . to the stars, really clear. I like this part. . . ."

Then, still in hypnosis, she exclaimed with sudden present-mind understanding and with both fear and amazement, "But this is death! This is *Death!*"

"Yes, and it's a lot different from what we thought, isn't it. Your body died, but you didn't; you floated up toward the stars and said, 'I like this part.'"

She came back to normal consciousness feeling a mixture of relief and amazement. We talked a little while longer in full consciousness, and when she left, she was smiling.

Few Limitations in the Altered State

In non-physical fields, as compared to the physical world, space and time have totally different meanings; it is almost as if they do not exist. When the therapist becomes familiar with the ability of the subconscious mind to move freely through both space and time, the process of psycho-expedition can be speeded up, the client moving smoothly from one life to another, for example, focusing chiefly on events that may have related to the formation of an attitude, a relationship, or an addiction. Merely perceiving the concat-enation of events leading to the client's present problem is helpful by itself, but with verbal assistance from the therapist in clearing the negatives and suggesting positive attitudes and habits, the therapeutic aspect is speeded up still more.

Another limiting concept of the physical world besides space and time is that each person's mind is his or her packaged possession. In hypnosis, however, the client's mind can easily contact the mind of any other person (or creature, for that matter) whether the contacted one is living or deceased. The therapist merely needs to request that the client contact the mind of so-and-so and carry on from there. The ethics of touching the private minds (invading the pri-vacy) of living persons needs to be considered carefully, but contacting the minds of persons deceased or the events or creatures of the past (the Akashic Records) is considered ethical. A person's puzzlements can be relieved by such contacts. For example, when one of my clients was not only able to relive her own feelings as she experienced her murder by a sister in a past life but could also contact the mind of her murderer as the act was committed and the thoughts and emotions of the sister afterward, both my client and I knew much more clearly what needed to be accomplished in order to free my client from her own hindering emotions, espe-cially now that she finds herself as a daughter of her former murderer.

A relatively straightforward session that I had in 1992 with a friend will illustrate how physical and psychological problems and attitudes may reappear life after life if not neutralized in some way.

Lanetta ("Johnnie") Carson, a retired Army nurse, was in her 80s at the time of this session, a vivacious active lady with memberships in many various organizations besides having a large garden and roomy house. Widowed, she lived alone with her dog and cat and could have had a quiet life when at home, but she grew enough in her garden to share with many friends and to can, dry, and preserve fruits and vegetables enough for an army, in addition to all her other activities. She had frequent headaches, a recurring neck problem that the chiropractor could alleviate only temporarily, and high blood pressure which prescribed drugs did not control. She was constantly on the go, aware of tension and a sense of urgency because "there's so much to do." She used self-hypnosis to great advantage in many aspects of her life but could not control these things with it. Friends kept telling her she needed to ease up the pressure and take life more calmly.

In hypnotic regression she was told to "Go to the basic cause or event related to your head and neck problems." Briefly, with pauses, she relived the event:

"I'm a young woman. . . . My name is Cora. It is England. I'm driving a horse and a fancy buggy. . . . Oh! The right wheel came off! I am thrown out . . . the right side of my head hits a rock—it shook up the inside of my head. . . . There's a blood vessel in the right side of my head that doesn't allow the blood to go through. . . .

"The accident killed me. I died from a broken neck. . . . I was *going too fast!*

"I don't want to die. There are so many things yet to do. . . . I hate to leave—I don't want someone else to get my husband. I have deep feelings for my husband, but I must go. . . . So he is *free*. . . ." (Tears were coming.)

After partially clearing this much by hypnotic techniques I directed her to go to the "superconscious level," back to the Planning State (see Glossary) for the life as Cora. She said her soul had chosen this family and had chosen to leave (to die) as an adult rather than as a child or a teenager. She wanted to live to be an old lady. She also found that this was not a true accident; the stable-man had not tightened the wheel enough after greasing it, and when he learned of the incident that killed her, he was devastated. She found nothing karmic in the event.

"Cora," I said, "you felt, 'There are so many things yet to do.' A very wise man asked me once, 'Why push? Is there not eternity?' So if you were not supposed to die until later and you left many things undone, there is still eternity in which to do them. Do you understand?"

She said she did, and I offered suggestions again that she ease up in the present life.

Then I directed her to go to the next life after Cora.

"I see myself talking," she said. "I'm a tall lady, a spinster. They are calling me a rabble-rouser. It is in the U.S., 1803; WOMEN'S RIGHTS TO VOTE! My name? All I get is 'Go get 'em!' I guess my name is Lydia. . . .

"I have to keep my hair cut short; it gets so heavy that it hurts my neck unless there is only a small bun on top; then there's no pain in my head. My heart pumps hard to get blood where it needs to go. Sometimes it just goes easily like water into a lake, but towards night there seems more of it, someone needs to *push* it along, and my head feels heavy. . . ."

I could see the patterning: Johnnie's neck problems were from traumata in her past lives, and her high blood pressure was from those past-life feelings of "Go get 'em," and "Too much to do."

Directed to see the last moments of her life as Lydia, she said she could see men standing behind the women to whom she had been lecturing. The husbands were telling their wives to get rid of her. On her way home as she was walking across a little bridge, some of the women came, smiling. She recognized them as some who had been against what she had said at the meeting that afternoon.

"They threw stones at me . . . left me on the bridge . . . walked away. I died soon after. My skull was broken on the right side—one woman had thrown a really good-sized rock. I don't die from the skull fracture but from exposure. It's November, and I'm not found until sunrise. . . . I didn't seem to care; it felt good to feel numb. I had no hatred for the. women. I only felt sorry they had to do what they did. . . ."

I offered Lydia more suggestions about "Doing what you can and letting the rest go," and about easing up. She was happy to hear that women now do have the vote.

"Good! It's been a long time coming!"

Then she was sent to the superconscious level (see Glossary) to look at this present life. She discovered that she no longer "needed" to have the headaches or the neck problem, and her own Higher mind advised, "Don't try to get everything done in one day."

As we read this little series of lives we note the repeated instances of pain in the right side of the head and in the neck, and the repetition of the feelings of hurry ("I was going too fast," and "There's so much yet to do")—and of incompletion. Bringing such subconscious awareness up to the conscious level is helpful by itself, but when combined with therapeutic suggestions from the facilitator and contact with the wisdom of the client's Higher Mind at the superconscious level, the result is still more effective. At present, however, Johnnie is still going hard and fast! She agrees that more therapy is needed for some of her problems, but she's "too busy." She is at least resting more now at 84, and her neck bothers her less. At times her blood pressure is low though still high at other times.

Definitions

Perhaps this is a good place to pause and explain some of the words used here. I shall be speaking of various "levels" of consciousness and of different parts of the mind:

The *conscious*, cognitive, reasoning mind, uses the left half of the brain in particular—analyzing, evaluating, figuring things out logically. It has been trained since we were in the First Grade to "listen!—concentrate!—think!—reason it out!"

The *subconscious* part of the mind is called by many the *unconscious*. I believe that Freud described it first for the modern Western world, although it has been known in other countries by other names for many centuries. It is a not-conscious part which is nevertheless always on the alert, even if the conscious part is sleeping or unconscious for any reason (anesthesia, concussion, drugs, etc.). Although it does not reason nor evaluate logically, and therefore is a poor master, it accepts commands and suggestions without questioning and tries to carry them out faithfully, and so is an excellent, powerful servant. It holds one hundred percent of a person's memories and the memory about everything and everyone that has had any relation to the person, including even the strong thoughts and emotions of other persons. It is the repository of both "good" and "bad" habits, attitudes, and patterns. It is not limited by space or time, and can contact all other subconscious minds.

The *superconscious* mind is also called by other names—e.g., the Higher Mind, the Higher Self, the Inner Mind, the Inner-Self-Helper, or the Soul. It is wise, perceptive, intuitive, and masterful and is focused on the spiritual and ethical growth of each person. Like the subconscious mind, it is not limited by space or time and can contact all other minds, and it contains all of a person's memories for all the past lives as well as the present life, and all the person's talents and potentials. It perceives and associates all events with the wisdom of understanding one's karma and one's overall purpose in life. In altered states of consciousness, it is contacted at the *superconscious level,* a dimension of wisdom, power, peace, insight, and love. At this level, a person in hypnosis may feel somewhat different from usual or may not; it seems not to matter. When requested, the Higher Self speaks through the hypnotized person's voice in third person with penetrating impersonal wisdom and understanding, always focusing on the importance of the spiritual aspects of each situation.

In an altered state, the subconscious and the superconscious levels can be accessed and brought to *conscious* awareness. The cognitive part of the mind is able to move easily from one level to the other, from present to past or future, and from place to place by following mild suggestions from a guide or therapist, while the *conscious part of the mind remains aware* of all that is happening—that is, present consciousness overlaps the sub- or superconscious aspects in what I call *blended consciousness.* This may be identical to what other writers have called "split" or "parallel" consciousness.

The word *spirit* has been used in two different senses for at least the past century. As used in the Spiritualist Church it means the disembodied personality and consciousness of a deceased person, that which left the body at death. Modern hypnotherapists use the term in this sense when they speak of the Releasement of a spirit from an obsessed person.

For other groups the word *soul* would probably be used in the above sense and *spirit* would be reserved as a synonym for the Superconscious Mind. Another definition of *spirit* in this sense is "that of God within," as Quakers call it—the divine part of every human being. One book states that "the spirit is housed in the soul, just as the soul is housed in the body." *(Mary's Message to the World,* Annie Kirkwood, 1993). This is close to the Theosophical definition.

I'll use a number of words—mind, soul, consciousness, psyche, personality—for the invisible parts of the self on the earth plane and astral level; and Superconscious Mind, Higher Mind or Higher Self and Soul (capitalized) when speaking of the high spiritual part of the total Self.

Universal Mind is another term used here. Universal Mind can be thought of as the sum total of all the laws of Nature: the laws of chemistry, physics, geology, astronomy, physiology—and also the laws of psychology. It may be considered the subconscious mind of the entire universe. Rolf Alexander, M.D. *(The Doctor Alone Can't Cure You,* 1948.) calls it the Framework of the Universe. Einstein might have called it *The Field:* the entire field of the whole physical universe, filled with light waves, gravitational forces, electromagnetic forces, and (as used in this work) also with thought-vibrations and vibrations of the emotions of all creatures—all of these being imprinted in permanent form in some way as *The Memory of Nature* (also called *The Book of Life* and *The Akashic Records).* Guided in an altered state of awareness, the human mind can contact these very simply and easily.

The Light is another term which many who meditate or who are in the work of hypnotherapy use. Dying persons may see the Light as their consciousness begins to become aware of higher vibrations, and in or near the Light the dying ones may see persons dear to them who have already died. Many of Dr. Moody's patients, after a Near Death Experience *(Life After Life,* 1973), speak of having seen a Light. They felt that the Light was living, intelligent, understanding, and totally loving and forgiving, "a being of light." Some felt that the Light was God. Christians, seeing the Light, may see a shining figure of Christ or Mother Mary. But Light represents universally a spiritual reality, the opposite of the darkness of ignorance, fear, evil.

You, too, will see it sometime—maybe before you die, maybe just as your body is dying. Maybe just afterward. You have something marvelous to look forward to.

For other definitions, please see the Glossary.

Philosophical Assumptions

For many readers to understand the material, it is necessary to become acquainted with certain concepts which are already familiar to others of you. For the present, knowing that to many these can be no more than mere concepts or theories, let us call them *Philosophical Assumptions:*

1. The physical body is a living vehicle for a living invisible mind. The physical body and brain will someday die and disintegrate; the mind, not made of physical material, does not die.

2. The mind is the living operator which uses the brain as a control-center through which it operates the body and contacts the outside world through the physical senses and affects it through the muscles.

3. The mind does not require a physical body or brain in order to be conscious and active. When the body and brain die, the mind retains awareness but is seldom able to affect the physical environment or contact physical beings satisfactorily.

4. Death is death of the physical body only, freeing the mind from the limitations of space and time but limiting its ability to communicate with embodied souls because it is now invisible and inaudible except to a small number (persons naturally psychic or in an altered state of consciousness).

5. The heritage of the physical body is the genetic inheritance of its genealogy, parents, grandparents, and on back through the generations, for hereditary strengths or for genetic or psychological weaknesses.

6. The heritage of the mind (consciousness, character, soul) is its psychospiritual inheritance—the result of all the past lives of the soul that have been developing talents and strengths or overcoming faults or weaknesses as the soul passed through many experiences.

7. The purpose of life in a physical body on this planet among physical forms appears to be that of training, educating, and developing the soul, i.e., the *character*, in psychospiritual ways.

8. Such training continues after the death of the body as the soul reviews the life just past, notes the incomplete parts, the strong and weak aspects, and judges itself. This is called the *Review* stage and the *Judging*.

9. The normal, rightful pathway for the newly disembodied mind, clothed still in its "astral body" of desires, emotions, and feelings, is to progress to the next plane or dimension, to enter a higher vibration—a state called the "next world" (not yet "heaven," although called so by those who do not differentiate the stages beyond death). Existence in this "astral world" is as normal and natural for disembodied minds (souls) as existence in the physical world is for physically embodied souls.

10. Each soul creates in the astral world its own environment of peace or pain according to what its activities in the earth life were, whether it created good or ill for its fellow beings. Each suffers what it caused others to suffer, enjoys what it enabled others to enjoy. No fiery hell of eternal torment has been discovered.

11. Many souls do not progress into the appropriate astral level at death, but remain *earth-bound* for various reasons, and many of these invade the physical bodies and obsess the minds of living persons, needing to be released so that they may be free to move on into the astral realm, and leave the embodied person free of the obsessing influence. The process is called *Releasement*.

12. A short or long period takes place between earth-lives, first in the astral world and then higher still in the mental planes, assimilating the wisdom and strength acquired during the earth-life just past and acquiring further learning and training.

13. When the soul is ready for another life on earth, it *plans* the coming life, usually with the assistance of wise discarnate counselors, before or shortly after the conception of the infant body. It may select its parents, or it may not. It may choose certain other conditions or be persuaded by the counselors to do so, in the best interests of developing the soul's spiritual resources. This is called the *Planning Stage*. If the soul does not wait to consult any counselors, it may unwisely jump back into incarnation into very undesirable circumstances.

14. Thus the soul *reincarnates*, bearing with it each time the "predispositions" (as Buddha called them) that were developed in previous lifetimes, and bringing also certain selected portions of its total karma to be worked on during the coming life: e.g., a sense of mission, a weakness to be overcome, a relationship to be reconciled, a talent to be developed, a love to be further matured, a debt to be balanced, and so on.

15. Evolvement continues life after life until the soul has become strong, steady, wise, and saintly. Then it may choose to go on to still higher spiritual fields or else remain close to embodied humanity as a Guide, a Teacher, or a Master, continuing to assist people on the earth-plane.

16. There is no perceivable end to this evolvement of the spirit. *There is no death except for the physical forms* of all creatures, which Nature *intends* to be recycled.

17. At all stages the soul has *free will* and may make its own choices. Its choice may prove to have been wise or unwise, but in either case the soul learns valuable lessons. Delays may result from unwise decisions and choices and

from self-limitations, but the ultimate result is the eternal progress of the soul.

Now, I know perfectly well that whereas some of you are following all these statements with nodding acceptance, others of you are shaking your heads in bewilderment or else in irritation because of the "lack of documentation." Dear friends, I cannot write for all of you in the words each might find most acceptable, so I am writing chiefly for those of you in grief or fear or who have a loved one who is threatened by death. The curious readers will at least find new thoughts in these pages, I think, and those of you who insist on references of "documentation"—well, I'll try to offer as much as is convenient. You know I am no longer a researcher but a therapist. I'm not attempting to prove anything here; I am simply writing what I have come to feel is authentic from my own previous experiences and from those of my hundreds of clients and patients over a good many decades. If this book bothers you, please forgive, and just toss the book aside—or into the waste basket. When you die—and that you will die is not something that needs much documentation—you may find out how much of this book turns out to be true and how much untrue. So just be patient, huh?

(Permit me a small chortle. I think you'll be pleasantly surprised!)

2

NEAR-DEATH
EXPERIENCES

UNTIL THE LAST FEW DECADES the stock objection to subjects relating to post mortem conditions was, "No one has ever died and come back to tell us about it." That is now changed.

Since the publication in 1975 of Dr. Raymond Moody, Jr.'s *Life After Life*, the term "near-death experience" has become well known and is in common usage, often abbreviated to "NDE." Moody listened when some of his college philosophy students told him of their activities and thoughts during a time when their bodies were "dead." He listened, and he heard rather similar stories over and over, after each of his public talks about these subjects. It seemed that the out-of-body experiences of many of the persons he interviewed were remarkably similar in a good many respects—too many respects to be coincidence or imagination. Such experiences occurred not only to persons apparently dead but also to many "who, in the course of accidents or severe injury or illness, came very close to physical death."

He was aware when he wrote the book that most of his medical colleagues would probably think that his data were "unscientific" and unreliable, but he had waited until he was quite certain that the phenomenon of the "near-death experience" was a common one before publishing his findings.

Moody was warned by Dr. Elizabeth Kübler-Ross to expect criticism not only from scientists and physicians but also from clergy, some members of whom are "upset by anyone who dares to do research on an area supposed to be taboo." He found support from her and from Dr. Kenneth Ring and others working in the same field of investigation who had heard similar stories from persons who had died and been resuscitated. These persons, "returned from the dead," insisted that they had not died but had left the body and, in full consciousness, had been able to move, usually as if floating, and had been able to think and feel emotions as if still in a body—but now a healthy body, not the injured or sick one that had "died."

Moody has written several more books on this subject. His list of the sensations and experiences reported in NDEs includes the following:

1. The person feels herself (or himself) sinking or relaxing, and hears the doctor or nurse say, "I'm afraid she's gone," or, "We've lost her."
2. She hears a loud buzzing or ringing noise,
3. and finds herself out of her body, floating, looking down at the body as an observer,
4. and feels that she is moving or being drawn through a tunnel.
5. She can see people working on the body, doctors and nurses, and can hear what they are saying. Her emotions may be in confusion or they may be calm.
6. She notices that she still has a body, in appearance like her physical body, but different in nature and powers.
7. She may see other persons coming toward her, relatives and friends who have died. They smile and greet her.

8 She also perceives a Light that is living, intelligent, and warmly loving, a Being of Light.

9. The Being of Light shows her a *review* of her entire life, as if instantaneously, and asks her (non-verbally) to *evaluate* the life in terms of spiritual gain or loss.

10. She perceives a barrier, such as a fence or a river, beyond which she is not able to go, for to do so would mean that she could not return to her body.

11. She is told by one of the beings or relatives that she must go back to earth, that it is not yet time for her to die.

12. She is resistant at first, regretting to leave the peace, love, and joyfulness of this sphere.

13. Nevertheless she is drawn back to the earth-plane and into her body, which begins to resume the various functions of life: the heart resumes beating, the respiration starts again, the patient may open her eyes or speak. Her body is alive.

14. Afterward she tries to tell friends and relatives of her experience, but they are incredulous or uninterested. She stops talking about the experience.

15. Still, the experience has influenced her deeply and permanently. She views life differently and finds that she has totally lost any former fear of death.

These are the recurring elements of an NDE. Not all these elements occur in any individual NDE, but each one is found over and over again among Moody's cases. Some patients recall more details than others do. And some persons have a dark or frightening NDE quite unlike the bright, joyous types commonly reported.

A Bright Near-Death Experience

A psychic friend of mine, Carroll Armstrong, wrote me the following story in 1994. All names and dates are real.

This experience that I am relating involves my extended family by marriage—it is about my sister-in-law's grandmother, Mrs. Morrissey. It happened a long time ago, and with the near-death experience came a prophecy that would be almost forty-five years old when fulfilled. I was told of this experience by Mrs. Morrissey when I was a teenager in 1961. She became my mentor. I was not afraid to share with her the psychic happenings in my life, and she in turn shared with me her experience.

Married at the age of 33, Mrs. Morrissey had her daughter, Mary Ethel, several years after that, in 1920. Her age, combined with a very serious post-partal infection, left little doubt that she would ever have another child. Over the next five years her health deteriorated; she could no longer teach at the business college or dance in their ballroom. The Morrisseys moved into a home that would accommodate the needs of Mrs. M, with quarters upstairs for nurses. (In 1925 people were still afraid to take loved ones to the hospital.)

At one time Mrs. M. was given her Last Rites by the priest and knew her life was ebbing away. She told me she was tired of the pain, tired of fighting. Her world became dark and she welcomed the peacefulness of death.

Then a beam of light pierced her place of darkness. A female figure appeared before her. Mrs. M. was sure that this figure was Mother Mary. Mrs. M. was told, "You cannot leave yet. You still have work to do on earth. You have two children to raise."

Mrs. M. protested. She was at peace and without pain. She did not want to go back to that pain-ridden sick body.

The female figure bathed in the bright white light again stated that Mrs. M. had a job to complete on earth, and it was to raise two children, and when that work was completed, she could come home. The figure then retreated into the light. (Or that could have been the impression from Mrs. M's point of view. It may have been that Mrs. M. was moving away from the light and headed back to earth.)

Mrs. M. saw a ribbon of light in the darkness before awakening in her fight for life. Written on the ribbon like a ticker-tape was the 23rd Psalm.

The daughter, Mary Ethel, married in May of 1942. She gave birth to two daughters, Mary Patricia (Patty) on February 2, 1943, and Judy on May 26, 1949. Mrs. M. led a very full, active, and healthy life from her wheelchair. Her daughter and two granddaughters lived with her for many years, occupying the house quarters that had been used by the nurses that took care of Mrs. M. in 1925.

It was Patty who introduced me to her grandmother in 1961, when she was dating my brother. Patty told me that Mrs. M. had been in a wheelchair for many years before Patty was born. I was pleasantly surprised to meet this well-dressed lady, every hair in place and make-up on, watching the St. Louis Cardinals' baseball game. At the beginning of the introduction she held up a gnarled hand and said, "Just a moment, please. I've got to see this play."

I liked her right off the bat, straightforward, honest, and self-assured. After the introduction she went right back to her baseball game. The Cardinals won, and Mrs. M. headed for the kitchen to cook supper. I followed, thinking she would need help. How wrong I was in that assumption. She asked me if I would like to stay for supper. She gave me a bit of knowledge that day. She showed me that people in a wheelchair could be just as efficient as anyone else in life.

Patty married my brother on January 4, 1964, and Judy was married April 12, 1969. I was at the reception of Judy's wedding in Mrs. M's home. Many people remarked that day, including myself, that Mrs. M. looked radiant. She had a glow about her. She was 85 years old but never had she looked so young in all the years I had known her. The unusualness of her appearance got as much attention as the bride.

Mrs. M. got sick a few days later. Two weeks after the wedding she told Patty in a long distance phone call, "I love you"—and she was on her way to the hospital. Three weeks to the day that her second granddaughter was married and in someone else's care, she took her scheduled flight into the light as promised, when her work on earth was done.

Mrs. M. had received communion on the anniversary of her vision every year until her death. The near-death experience happened in 1925, and the prophecy was fulfilled in 1969. The St. Benedict's Catholic Church in Atchison, Kansas, recorded the incident.

A Darker Near-Death Experience

An example of the darker type of NDE is the story of "Hal," the husband of one of my friends, who in his younger years was a crude, insensitive fellow who chased around a good deal. He hired himself out as a farmhand and married the sixteen-year-old orphan girl who was helping out in the house for her room and board. She became pregnant almost at once, was alone most of the months of pregnancy because he was somewhere else, and gave birth to her first child at the age of seventeen, alone except for a midwife. Nor was he present for the births of his other three children in the years following.

As the decades passed, however, he became less self-centered and thoughtless. He was middle-aged when I first met him, and I came to like him.

In the 1970s he developed a pneumonic condition that worsened rapidly. His doctor sent him to a hospital, and with his wife, I visited him there one evening. He recognized me. His lips moved. When I leaned close, he whispered, "I don't see . . . how a fellow can . . . be *so tired* . . . and still breathe."

I told his wife that I felt he could not live through the night. "Usually the body's resources are lowest in the hours after midnight. I think he may go around two or three o'clock in the morning." She nodded. He seemed to lapse into coma.

In the morning, however, he was alive and stronger—which just goes to prove that doctors do not know everything! Hal continued to improve and soon became strong enough to return home.

While he was recovering I visited him and happened to speak of near-death experiences, mentioning that a man had reported after an NDE that he had seen a dark, dank cave-like place, not the bright scenes that many report seeing.

Hal interrupted, "That's where I was." He described a dark cave with water trickling down the rough walls, stale smells in the thick air, and "things" clinging to the walls and floating through the air.

"Things?" I questioned.

"Yeah, *things*—like bats, or big crabs, just sticking on the walls and ceilings, and *things* floating in the air—just . . . *things*." Not nice things, apparently, if one judged from his grimace.

I found myself saying, "Hal, I think that was a vision of the type of place you might have gone to if you had died in the hospital. But I think your recovery is the gift of another chance."

Hal accepted this interpretation soberly.

He lived for two or three years after this. I noticed that he was more thoughtful of his wife, that he smiled and joked more often, that he seemed to have come to terms with life in general in spite of the terrible headaches that sometimes almost blinded him and the back problems that caused him pain.

His death was from the sudden rupture of an abdominal aneurysm which, like the headaches, might have been one result of his old tertiary syphilis. When the rupture occurred, his wife said later that he doubled over with the pain, asked her to help him to the bed, and gasped, "Honey, I wish I could stay, but I can't." In a very few minutes he lost consciousness.

She phoned me in panic, and I drove the several miles to their country cabin to find her distraught and him already dead. Again she had been alone in a time of great stress— unless, of course, his consciousness had remained near, trying to comfort her. Neither she nor I could be aware of that, however.

She had been a faithful church member; he had not attended any church. The minister of her church nevertheless officiated at his burial and gave a sympathetic talk, reminding the people who had gathered of how Hal had helped out with church projects in various ways: carpentry, landscaping, etc. I wondered if Hal had stayed around long enough to attend his own burial. I felt that, if so, he was pleased to have his work appreciated.

A Near-Death Experience and Ethical Transformation

During a near-death experience there is often a sense of the interconnectedness between one's self and other beings, a sense that one experiences the other beings' thoughts and feelings intimately, as one's own. Dr. David Lorimer, director of the Scientific and Medical Network in England, says, "This has far-reaching ethical implications. It means that whatever we do to others we are really in the end doing to ourselves."

During ordinary life experiences this rule may not seem to be obvious. Intellectually one may believe in the law of Universal Justice, called Karma, but when justice seems to be delayed, the remembrance of the law fades from consciousness. Great teachers through the ages have told us that whatever we do comes back to us, whether good or ill.

Buddha expressed it as, "Do not unto others as you do not want others to do to you." We have called this "The Silver Rule." The well known "Golden Rule," taught by the Buddha and also by the Carpenter of Galilee, is the positive form: "Do unto others as you would like them to do to you."

Dr. Lorimer gives an example of the transformative effect of the life-review in the NDE of a man who had been in prison repeatedly for serious crimes.[2] Believing that time spent in sick-bay would be less unpleasant than in the usual prison routine, he ate a quantity of soap, which produced a severe inflammation of the intestine with acute pain. While this condition lasted, through the next several weeks he saw his life repeatedly, including, besides the criminal acts he had committed, also all the small injuries he had inflicted on others by his thoughts, words, and deeds.

Not only did he review all these things, but, in his own words, "The most terrifying thing about it was that, as the scroll unwound, every pain and suffering I had caused to others was now felt by me. You can imagine the kind of searingly painful experience this would be. My experience was extreme—most of us are not in this category—but all of us have our own litany of injustices we can relate to."

After about a dozen repetitions of this painful reliving of his life, he began to come to terms with his inner self during the four months that he was kept in isolation. His experiences became like those of his childhood dreams, of being in a garden receiving love and nurturing. Like many people who become criminals or embittered, he had come from a loveless family and had no patterning for tenderness.

Then came a third state, when "for the first time I had a joyous sense of bestowing love . . . I loved everyone; I hated only the evil conditions people had imposed on each other

---

[2]From a talk given at The Institute of Noetic Sciences Conference, Chicago, 1994. Printed in the *Noetic Sciences Review*, Winter, 1994.

and upon themselves." As the scroll of his life unrolled again there was no pain in it. As each person came before his consciousness he sent that person love, which soothed their hurts. "All the people who had been injured by me appeared. One by one, I began to help them and love them. It was exceedingly vivid."

Apparently the NDE that this man experienced during the first acute stages of his illness triggered an ongoing process of similar life-reviews that might not technically be near-death experiences. Nevertheless, they fit easily into the mystical and metaphysical experiences of the psyche that are reported by other persons who have had NDEs.

Dr. Lorimer comments, "Perhaps the most profound implication of the near-death life review is that everything we do, think, and feel is, in some way, recorded—an insight insisted on by many of the great spiritual masters through the centuries."

This record-in-toto has been called the Memory of Nature, or the Akashic Records. It has been called the Book of Life. Whatever its nature, it provides a complete story of the facts of history and forms the basis of the law of nature that says that whatever we do to others comes back to us, for good or ill: "With what measure you mete, it shall be measured to you again"; "Whatsoever you sow, that you shall also reap," to quote the Galilean Teacher again.

Another Transformative NDE

A near-death experience vastly different from that of the criminal's is Minette Crow's, but hers is like it in the sense of intimate connectedness between the individual and other beings.

When I wrote to ask Minette for permission to quote her letter (which I had read in a 1993 "Travel Program" of the

Institute of Noetic Sciences), her husband answered for her, saying that she gladly gave her permission but was barely able to write herself, because of a bilateral stroke which she had in 1994. At present, he added, she is improving gradually. I received the impression that she is quietly accepting the events of her life, with the care and help of her husband, and is ready for whatever the next stages may be.

This is her published letter:

The first time I left my body was during a near-death experience (NDE) that completely changed my former understanding of existence and gave me many reasons to re-enter my body to continue this life. Here is a small portion of (that) NDE that transformed my thinking:

As I moved upward, the light grew larger and brighter until it burst upon me, and I was completely enveloped in its blinding radiance. Somehow, I knew this must be God, for I experienced overwhelming love, peace, and joy. I was alone in this light for what seemed only a moment, but I could feel its pulsations like the surge of a gigantic heart, vitalizing me into a brilliance like its own, for I had been dissolved into that light! I was still "me" and could think as "me"—and yet I became a different individual from the one who had entered the hospital, because I understood a new meaning to this word *light*. God was Light and *that* Light had within it everything anyone would want to know. I don't mean to say I *learned* all there was to know, but I realized that any kind of special knowledge was there within the Light.

The brilliance seemed to recede somewhat and became a permeating, effulgent glow. I discovered that I had been transported to another dimension where there were souls who, like me, had left their bodies on Earth. They greeted me with indescribable love, and I recognized two whom I'd known previously. One was my father, who had died several years earlier, and the other was my grandmother who had died when I was fourteen. No longer old and full of pain, they appeared to be in the prime of life and full of joy, just as I was.

The others I didn't recognize as people I'd known on Earth, yet I knew them, they knew me, and I loved them as they loved me. All of us were in the light of that love, no longer separate and alone the way each person seems to be on Earth, but each of us made up a part of the whole, which was one. I now understand what one great illuminate meant when he said, "I and my Father are one." In other words, I felt I had re-entered the womb of creation where I had begun this earthly life. I was now returning to that same beginning, which could also be the end of my earthly existence.

A musical sound—human in voice quality—came from each of us, who had his or her own tonal octaves. Yet, all merged into a joyful chorus of harmonizing sound. To understand this, one would have to imagine that as you think, you emit a rhapsodic tone that is as beautiful as your thought and that each person's thoughts merge into one vast, harmonic symphony. Instead of *saying* the word "love," our thoughts create a tonal note that means the same thing.

Suddenly, without warning, I heard a noise like static on a radio that is interrupting a symphony of harmonic beauty. I heard somber, dismal tones that were at once strident and sad. It disturbed me so deeply that I began to weep.

"What is that *horrible* noise?" I asked.

"It is the combined thought-tones of millions on Earth," they replied.

I knew that I was being taught and shown things I had never thought of before. "But why aren't the rest of you weeping?"

"Because we know those on Earth will not always have such tones."

"How long will it take to hear a harmonious sound?"

"As long as it takes people of Earth to realize they are one with each other and think love instead of hate."

I wept again. "It will take a long time."

"Yes," they said, "but you can help by telling what you're learning here."

These four examples of Near-Death Experiences give an idea of the variation in such experiences. For most ordinary decent people the NDE is an event of peace and beauty beyond words and provides the experiencer with a complete trust in the beauty of death, whenever death may come. Fear of death has been totally abolished by the experience. Yet, although there may be a longing to return to that state of peace and beauty and love, there is also a profound recognition of the value and beauty of life in the physical world, of its sacredness, *not* to be thrown away through suicide or murder.

For any of us who have habitually been self-centered and cold-hearted, the NDE may be a cold, unpleasant type of experience, such as Hal's, or even like the "searingly painful" life-review that the long-time criminal had. It is our own subconsciousness that decides the sort of NDE that will appear as a symbolic representation of the contents of our deep self, past and present, and of the type of future we have been preparing for ourselves. It is therefore a warning, and also a message of hope: "Look at what you have been doing to yourself by what you have been doing or thinking toward others. You need to change!" Even the hardened life-long criminal changed completely during those painful weeks when he had to look honestly at all the suffering he had caused others and to suffer the pains himself.

I like to think (and I believe this is true) that it is a person's Higher Self, his or her Soul on the Superconscious level, that oversees and supervises such painful NDEs, allowing the soul on the lower level to suffer only as much as it can bear,

and prolonging the process if necessary rather than overwhelming the lower consciousness with a shorter but more
brutal experience of what the Soul has caused others to
endure.

A Near-Death Experience can be considered a foretaste
of what each soul can expect after the physical body really
does die. Each soul prepares its own after-life conditions by
the "material" it sends to the astral plane—the thoughts,
emotions, desires, attitudes, and actions. This eventuates in
complete *justice*—although one is reminded of Kipling's
tongue-in-cheek lines in "The Gods of the Market Place":

> Where each one insists on his merits,
> And no one desists from his sins. . .

We would all like to get full credit for our good points and
avoid payment for our sins and weaknesses! If we ourselves
are our judges and executioners, however, we can always
change ourselves and direct ourselves toward a happier
future. It is not true that Opportunity knocks but once. There
is always new opportunity! A person may not make his
change as dramatically and suddenly as Scrooge did, but the
Opportunities keep coming and coming. Each morning is a
new day, and, as Buddha told people, "Every day is a good
day to begin the [better] life."

Because this is a book not about Near-Death but about
Death, these four illustrative NDEs will be enough here.
They state that people do die or come very near death and
come back to tell about it.

3

ASSISTED TRANSITION

ASSISTED TRANSITION, a death process helped along by scientific, religious, or other means, can be considered in several categories: First, those cases of *euthanasia* in which the patient is helped to leave the body by *chemical means*—very deep anesthesia, the administration of drugs, or the injection of a lethal amount of cyanide or other chemical substance. This procedure is, of course, desired first of all by the patient and is assisted by a sympathetic physician who has the understanding and consent of the patient's relatives.

In the U.S. the name of Dr. Jack Kevorkian has achieved great publicity for his work of aiding victims of Alzheimer's disease and other incurable conditions to die before they lose their mental faculties and become dependent. Critics have called him "Doctor Death"—a bitter, unfair name for a physician whose purpose is to relieve the fears and prevent the deterioration of the desperate persons who request his help to die. Neither he nor these patients have a fear of the body's death. Some of his critics, on the other hand, may have such a fear or feel that physical life is far preferable, even in its painful helpless terminal stages, to death—which to them may mean total annihilation of the self. Some doctors admit to feeling a sense of personal failure when a patient dies, as if their inability to keep the patient alive diminishes their standing with their peers and their feeling of professional competence.

In our meditation group we asked one time about the doctors in the Netherlands, whose activities in the field of euthanasia are fairly wide-spread and becoming rather widely known. Through a channel a firm calm voice told us, *"If the doctors have compassion they will receive compassion."* There was no indication that the use of euthanasia for persons requesting death for valid, carefully considered reasons was either sinful or unethical.

The doctors need to be aware, of course, that a jealous relative or a greedy heir-in-line might try to convince either the patient, the doctor, or both, that the patient is ripe for removal from the earth-scene. The doctors also need to be motivated by compassion and no lower motive. Here now, as many times before, we seem to be told, "There is no absolute rule. Each individual case needs to be evaluated for itself. Sometimes the answer is yes, sometimes no, for the best *spiritual* result."

Psychospiritual assistance offers another form of aid for transition, in which quietness, soft music, perhaps mantras or chanting, soft lights (especially orange lights, but only when death is close), help to provide a calm, soothing environment as the consciousness of the dying person prepares itself to vacate the sick, hurt, or outworn body. The intrusion of flurry and bustle, of needles and injections, of electric jolts, of pumping on the chest, of cries for a nurse, a doctor, or for the patient himself to remain—all of these disturb the dying person's consciousness as he gradually withdraws his attention from the body. Some souls contacted after death admit to feelings of strong resentment, even anger, at being bombarded by such distracting procedures as these.

A different sort of disturbance was reported by Drew Pearson, who at one time was one of the nation's top news commentators, along with Walter Winchell, a rival on another station. Winchell's manner was flamboyant. Many of us recall the way in which he would announce some bit of news: "FLASH! Today there is _____ " etc.

One time Pearson was in the hospital seriously ill. The small radio at his bedside was playing soft music. He said he felt himself floating away, blissfully aware of nothing but freedom and that heavenly music . . . when suddenly the music was interrupted by a loud voice: "FLASH! Drew Pearson is at the point of death in such-and-such hospital. He will be dead by morning!"

Drew said that he recognized Winchell's voice and became so irritated at the prediction that he vowed he would prove Walter wrong! He dragged himself away from the heavenly music and returned to his sick body and lived to tell the story. (1 wish I could remember where I heard this story. Please write me if you know more about it. Was Drew sorry that he came back? I do not recall, but I remember that he felt pleased to have proved his rival's prophecy wrong!)

In Eastern monasteries various physical methods are known that assist the transition of the consciousness when the body is ready to be put aside. Some involve pressure on certain nerves. Such knowledge is too dangerous to be given as yet to the public, for it could be easily distorted or misused in experiments or in moments of anger. "A little knowledge is a dangerous thing," wrote the poet: With a little knowledge, but not enough, a child could easily "experiment" on a pet or younger sibling; a teenager might boastfully attempt a sort of Russian Roulette game with teen friends; and so on.

We ourselves have utilized other methods of assisting the transition of a patient. One method was discovered by my friend Lanetta Carson, a retired Army nurse. When attending the bedside of an elderly friend, Lanetta mentally visualized a capsule of rainbow colors surrounding the sick woman and suggested that Marie take from it whichever colors, with their symbolic meanings, were needed to ease her body. Several times during her visits to Marie, Lanetta "put the rainbow around her." She said that sometimes Marie took one color, sometimes a different one, as seen by Lanetta clairvoyantly. Then one day Lanetta saw the capsule of all the colors become plastered closely to Marie's body as if skin-tight. Lanetta was puzzled. Marie's death occurred shortly thereafter—a few hours.

Some years later Lanetta attended Marie's middle-aged son as he lay in pain with his disease. Again Lanetta "put the rainbow around him" repeatedly. Again there came a time when he seemed to draw all the colors tight around his body, just as his mother had. This time Lanetta wondered if it meant that the moment of death was close. It was: only about a day.

One thinks of the observation of clairvoyants, who say that the absence of an aura presages imminent death. In one instance, a group of people seen to be without auras entered an elevator and died as a group when the elevator fell. In another case, a prominent man died one night of a heart attack at a conference I was attending, and afterward several people mentioned having seen no aura around him the evening before.

A method that I have used a number of times is the *pre-programming* of a client for his or her eventual transition, using hypnosis to speak directly to the subconscious mind.

The first patient whom I decided to program hypnotically in this way was a mentally retarded little woman with many severe birth defects and much pain from ever-increasing arthritis in neck, limbs, spine, and hands. She had lost her usual cheery disposition. The nurses hurt her whenever they lifted her from the recliner chair in which she lived by day.

They hurt her when they bathed her. Sobbing, she told me of her pain and discouragement.

I placed her in hypnosis, thinking only to give suggestions to mitigate the pain. Then it occurred to me to add programming that she herself could use, either as posthypnotic suggestions or, eventually, to control to some degree her actual passing.

"And whenever you feel that it is the right time, just ask the angels to lift you out of your troubles. If it isn't the right time, the only thing that will happen is that you will feel easier, more comfortable and peaceful, and the nurses' hands will make you feel better with every touch. But if it is the right time, then you will find yourself floating up and looking down at your body. You will feel light and happy and free. You will be able to walk if you want to, or run, or even fly. You will be out of that body that has held you confined."

If this sounds too beautiful, remember that from my own death experiences and those of many others who have described their deaths, this is almost exactly what does happen. I spoke to poor crippled "Retta" (with the twisted thorax, the laboring heart, the warped neck and spine, the useless legs and surgically stiffened wrists) as my heart and also my mind instructed. I *believed* what I told her. What I was not sure of was the exact time that was the "right time" for her.

I had told her family that if she got another attack of pneumonia, it would probably take her, but that I preferred not to send her to the hospital, to be stuck with needles in her little collapsed veins. After a moment of anger at my decision, the family understood. While I was briefly out of town, however, Retta was hospitalized by the attending physician when she developed lung congestion. She died in the hospital a few days later before I returned. I went to her burial and met her parents, brothers, and sisters. We talked. Although they belonged to a religious group that usually disapproves of hypnosis, they understood what I had done for Retta and expressed appreciation. We all felt that the little defective body had let go the imprisoned mind and Retta was free at last.

The next patient I programmed was a mentally retarded man, who according to his own words, "Fell down the stairs when I was a kid and it knocked all the sense out of me"— probably quoting his older brother, whom he adored. Teddy was always hyperactive, hobbling around the halls of the nursing home, hardly able to be quiet long enough to be induced into a restful hypnotic trance. When I found him in a hypoglycemic stupor one time, however, I used the opportunity to program him in much the same manner as I had programmed Retta. His brother was dead by now, and his only living relative was the sister-in-law, who had always expressed resentment towards him. I felt that his only real friends were the nurses of the care center. Again it was while I was out of town that the "right time" came. The nurses found his body, still warm, lying quietly in his bed. On his chart I had written that "no heroics" were to be used in the event of a deterioration in his general condition. In my programming to him I had mentioned that his mother and his brother would be waiting for him whenever the "right time" came for him. (These were suppositions on my part. Often it is indeed the mother who comes to accompany the newly arrived soul to the next dimension; sometimes it is another relative or friend.)

A third person I pre-programmed was a dear friend of mine, Edith Cox, a widow, who had developed an extremely painful bone condition that included deterioration of the spine. Trained in self-hypnosis, still Edith was unable to control the terrible pain. On a visit to her nursing home, I asked if she would like me to give her some extra hypnosis to help out her own programming. She gladly assented. But my suggestions only seemed to make matters worse, in spite of all the positive terms I could think of. She struggled to her feet, gasping, "Maybe it will help if I walk," and staggered back and forth.

I was at my wits' end, totally confused and bewildered. This had never happened before. Silently I called into the higher dimensions for more wisdom as how to help her. And the thought occurred to me that since she was a caring person and this was a nursing home where others were no doubt in pain, she might have absorbed some of the others' pains.

Starting with this idea, I commanded that any pain that did NOT belong to her body leave at once—not to return to wherever it came from, but to go outside and dissipate as a harmless vapor that would bother no living creature, human or nonhuman.

She became quieter as I was speaking, lying and breathing softly as I continued, "And any pain that does belong to your body is now coming into your left little finger and swelling it up until it has had enough" (I did not know how much "enough" was)—and then just pinch off the left little finger and put it in the drawer over there. Now do the same with the right little finger. . . ." She was deeply relaxed now; this Ericksonian method of dissociation was effective.

I asked if she wanted me to program her for passing, whenever that might be. She nodded, and I went on, "Any last lessons that you need to learn in this life you will learn easily and quickly. And any last tasks that you need to do you will be able to accomplish beautifully and completely, so that you feel satisfied. And when you feel that the right time has come, just tell yourself to lift out of your body. If it is not the right time for you, the only thing that will happen is that you feel easier, more quiet, patient, and peaceful in mind and more comfortable in body. . . ." and so on.

She was very deep in hypnosis, very quiet. I leaned over and asked softly if she would like to remain relaxed as she was. When she nodded, I told her I would leave my roses and go. She opened her eyes slightly and whispered, "Thank you," with a little smile, and I tiptoed out. It was the last time I saw her.

She had wanted to move to a nursing home several miles away. When a vacancy was available in the second nursing home, the administrator phoned to let me know, and I called Edith's nursing home. I learned that she was not there. She had fallen, broken her wrist, and was in the hospital. I called the hospital and gave my message to a nurse, asking for Edith's reply as to whether she still wanted to move. Her answer, yes, she wanted to take the vacancy.

In the afternoon the administrator called again. "Well, Louise, your little friend didn't make it."

"My little friend? Which little friend?"

"The little lady who you said wanted this empty bed. She died this morning."

"Died? Why, I was talking through a nurse to her at 8:30 this morning!"

"She passed away at 10:00."

My rational mind started thinking. Edith could have fallen and hit her head. She could have over-reacted to a medication and gone into anaphylactic shock. She could have had a heart attack or a stroke. However, I felt that she had been reminded of her programming by my phone call and used her own power to release herself, knowing that there was no useful future for her poor aging body with its painful wrist and spine. I believed she helped herself, and chose the "right time" to go.

For some reason I hesitated to investigate, even to ask the hospital what had happened. I wondered if it were ethical, or perhaps a sort of invasion of her privacy or mere curiosity, if

I were to ask a lot of questions that actually were not very important.

Now, however, for the purposes of this book, I shall ask a co-worker to help and I shall call Edith to let us know about her sudden passing.

Several years have gone by since Edith "didn't make it" to the nursing home. Yesterday evening, April 19, 1995, Susan McGinness and I made time for a session purposely to ask if it was permissible for Edith to come and tell us about her passing. (In the ESP class, Nan Taylor had taught us to think of our deceased friends as still *people*. "They don't suddenly become angels just because they died. They are people who are busy with their own activities and interests. We need to be polite when we invite them to return to this heavier realm to talk with us. We are told to give them a little notice of our intention and to ask if such a contact is permissible. It is not courteous for us to jerk them down to our earth-plane without warning or without asking first.")

Susan was facilitating, and I went into hypnosis.

S: (after deepening Louise until her "Yes" finger said the depth was sufficient) Is it permissible for us to call Edith Cox's Higher Self and talk with her? (finger: "Yes.")

S: Why did you choose that time?

E: I just wanted to go. . . . I thought it was the right time earlier—but I was *sure* that this was the "right time."

S: Did Louise's programming help?

E: I had forgotten it. She programmed me when I was very deep in hypnosis, and she left me still deep in hypnosis. I forgot it. [There is usually more or less amnesia after a period in hypnosis, especially if the depth was greater.] The telephone call reminded me of the programming. It all came back gradually.

S: Were you able to use the programming?

E: Yes, as soon as the nurse left me, I began thinking and it came back slowly. I wasn't sure exactly how to do it. So I experimented.

S: What worked best?

E: Well, I knew Emerson—my husband—wanted me to come. I called him and asked him to help me remember my programming. I saw him—he was smiling. I asked him, "How should I do it?" He said, "Just *come*." He always thought things were so simple! I didn't know how to "just come." And then I began to remember, to put myself into self-hypnosis . . . and program myself to rise up, to float up and out. And it was so simple! (laughing) I laugh because it was *so easy!* I thought it might be hard. (Susan laughing, too. Louise, as channel, feeling Edith's laughter bubbling up irrepressibly within her).

S: Could Louise have made the program better, changed the words so they helped more?

E: The words were all right. Louise didn't know how *simple* it was. Emerson was right, that it was simple and easy, but he didn't tell me how to do it. Louise did tell me how. It was so light! . . . I couldn't help laughing when the nurse came back. She was so upset! She wondered if it was something she had done or not done. Poor girl! I was so happy, so free! Emerson told me not to worry about her, that there was nothing to show she had done anything wrong. It was the "right time" . . .

Emerson learned something, also. He learned patience. When he wanted me to come over before, Louise told him he needed to wait until it was my time. She *told* him. Emerson didn't like to be *told* by anyone, but she's one that could. (laughter)

L: Well, I told him gently—but firmly! (more laughter)

E: She was right when she programmed me that if there was anything I needed to learn before I left my body, I would learn it easily, and if there was any task I needed to finish, I would be able to complete it satisfactorily and would feel pleased with it. Emerson's sister felt that I had not completed my last task, clearing out the house. It was a heavy burden for her to do it. I'm sorry. It was one of those tasks I *couldn't* do with my feeble body. For love of Emerson, his sister did it.

S: Do you have any further advice for people who are dying?

E: I was programmed to use hypnosis to put myself into an altered state, but people don't have to depend on hypnosis. When they feel it is the "right time" and they have done all they could to clear out things so that others won't have a great deal to do, and they are sure that dying is not just a selfish thing, then when they truly believe, spiritually, that it is time, just say a prayer, and ask to be lifted up or, as I did, call someone (deceased) who can come to help. If it is their time, it will be easy. If it is selfish or if they are trying to escape from work that is properly theirs, then it isn't the right time.

The journey is not "far." I didn't have to come from a long distance to come tonight. It is more like changing gears, from a high gear to low . . . Emerson is here too. He would like to "get even" with Louise. (laughing)

L: (in hypnosis as channel, now speaking as herself): Just wait until I come over. He will have plenty of opportunity. (More laughter)

S: We want to thank you for coming and telling us these things.

E: It's been a pleasure for us to help.

S: Is there any advice for Louise as she works on the book?

E: She knows what she should do, but she lets herself be distracted by the many earthly things; then she reproves herself and then she pushes herself harder.

Emerson says, "Just DO it!" (Laughing) Emerson says he's "gotten even" with Louise. (Louise sees Emerson as the large, self-assured imposing person he had been in life, this time with an impish sparkle in his eyes and a very self-satisfied expression, like a cat that ate the canary.)

L: Okay, I will.

S: And I'll see that she does! (More laughter, as L. returns to full consciousness.)

A fourth case in which I assisted was that of a young woman who had been my student in several hypnosis courses. When I returned from a trip, I learned that Linda was in the hospital, diagnosed with "oat-cell" cancer of the lung, a rapidly growing non-smoker's type of cancer. Amazed, I hurried to visit her. She was despondent, full of the doctors' predictions as to the remaining time of her life: six weeks, they had said.

I was angry. The doctors had been sincere, I had no doubt, but they had "programmed" her negatively, and she had, as I told her emphatically, "swallowed their programming, hook, line, and sinker!" Right there in the hospital room I began to cancel out those negatives and offer strong positive programming: first for stasis of the lesions, then for gradual shrinking and absorption. (The subconscious mind has incredible power!)

She went home in a few days and I visited her once there. The next time, she drove to my home, a trip of some twenty-four miles one way. Again I gave her solid programming for returning health.

She began to think of taking a trip with her husband from Colorado to Chaco Canyon in New Mexico to see her son by a former marriage. I was doubtful of the wisdom of the trip, but she went anyway, became very tired, partly because of family problems down there, and returned in renewed despondency.

I offered more programming. To my surprise, she was reluctant. I accused her directly of quitting, of giving up. This I knew was a challenge, for she was very "Indian" in many ways, an echo from her previous life as a chieftain. This time, however, she did not respond to my needling. Sighing, she said she thought it would be better for her to die.

I offered to compromise with her. We would contact her own Higher Self in hypnosis and accept whatever her Higher Self said was the wisest path. Her husband and I had already agreed to respect her decision not to have the chemotherapy. She had taken one course of radiation at the first diagnosis and agreed to another course later. I felt that she had about a fifty-fifty chance of recovery.

Her Higher Self seemed to agree, saying that the decision would be made by her conscious mind: that she could choose either to live or to die, but emphasized that she needed to complete her life-lesson by ceasing to control other people. If she lived, her lessons would include learning to let her husband and daughter have more freedom of choice and learning that she could not control all the circumstances of her life, such as financial income. If she chose to let her body die now, these lessons would still have to be learned in a future time.

Linda felt that her life-long habits were too strong to be changed without terrific stress in this life and she did not feel equal to the effort. She chose to let go and allow her body to deteriorate. I admit that as a doctor and a friend as well, and also as her teacher of self-hypnosis, I was a bit disappointed in her decision, but like her husband, I did respect her choice as one of her free will. She had lived a full six months since the prognosis of six weeks had been made. Now she faded quickly. I visited her several times at her home to give some relief from pain.

Toward the last, Linda asked for me to come. I programmed her for passing, telling her in the presence of her husband how it would be: "You will lift out of your body and see it on the bed below you. You will be in your astral body now.

"The astral body is attached by a silvery cord to the physical body, usually from the solar plexus or the heart region, sometimes from the head. As long as this cord is intact, you can still get back into the physical body, perhaps for one last smile or one last squeeze of the hand. But if the cord is broken, the body is really dead and you cannot return to it."

She asked me to program that she leave the body right then, for the pain was extreme. I answered, "No, this might not be the right time for you. We need to wait for your own time." (From the perspective of several years later, however, I feel that my decision was cold and insensitive. If I had the opportunity to relive the moment, I would have helped her right then, as the nurse also wanted me to.)

In two more days, Linda died. Our mutual friend, the nurse, was with her and awakened her husband to come for the last breaths. The actual passing was quiet. Linda's face was so relaxed that her mouth was slightly open. Later the nurse tried to close it but was unable to do so. She was surprised when the husband commented, "I see you got her mouth closed. I tried to but couldn't."

"No, I thought you had closed it," rejoined the nurse.

Both agreed that on Linda's face was a sweet, peaceful smile. Had Linda recalled my programmed thought that until the Silver Cord is broken, the consciousness can be returned to the body "perhaps for one last smile," and she had come back in to close the mouth? And perhaps her return was in answer to her husband's wish, overheard by the nurse after Linda's death, "My sweet woman, I wish I knew that you are all right. . . ."

At Linda's request there was no funeral. She had taken considerable interest in planning how her burial should be, telling her husband and daughter that she wanted no embalming, just to be dressed in her usual garments but with small items that would be reminders of her dogs, her horses, and her family. She wanted to be buried under some huge old cottonwood trees on the home property, and the special permit had already been obtained. Thelma, the nurse, attended the simple burial and told me of its simplicity and beauty.

In a fifth example of hypnotically assisted transition, it was a co-worker, Charlene Smith, R.N., who helped her mother through death. At my request, she wrote of her mother's passing.

My mother, Grace Compton, was a very active person—busy with church work, club work, yard work, and just enjoying life. In her later years her health wasn't very good. She especially hated having to use a cane or walker because of her arthritis, but she still kept busy. In January, 1984, she was diagnosed as having untreatable cancer. She continued to be as active as possible. As a Registered Nurse and a hypnotherapist, I helped her some, but when she needed more help with pain control, I referred her to my friend, Dr. Louise Ireland-Frey. Louise helped her with pain control at this time, and also gave her the suggestion that there was a "quiet little river with a gentle current" to cross when she was ready.

By May my mother was in the hospital in terminal condition and because of the medication was unable to respond part of the time. I was unable to talk with her much of the time. I was with her when she started having Cheyne-Stokes respirations [see Glossary]. She was so ill and seemed so restless that I was not sure hypnosis would help, but decided to try to help her "cross over."

I reminded her of the river that she could cross when she was ready. This river, I said, was in a beautiful setting. If she wanted to, she could walk or wade across, because it wasn't deep and the water was comfortably warm. The scenery on the other side was more beautiful than on this side of the river. [Charlene was using hypnotic suggestions here, as a guided meditation.] I also told her that although there were people who would miss her here, they realized that there were dear ones on the other side who were waiting to greet her. I told her that I could not see who would be there, but she could see them. And when she wanted, she could cross the river and *run* to meet them on legs that were pain-free and strong again.

Mother's breathing became calm and her body seemed more relaxed after this. She remained like this until shortly before she died the next day, when she opened her eyes and spoke normally for a little while with the family members who were with her. Then she again appeared to be relaxed and at peace.

These instances of how we have assisted people with hypnotic programming are enough to show you the general approach: to aid the dying person to a calm, expectant attitude, willing to go on without reluctance or fear, secure in the knowledge that the transition is being monitored and smoothed by a friend or relative so that the dying person does not feel alone and is not disturbed or prodded to respond in any way.

As Edith Cox pointed out when we called her back to get her input, hypnosis is by no means necessary. Any compassionate person can assist a terminal person in much the same way. During the last hours the patient's mind is open to suggestions almost as if he or she is in an altered state, and quiet suggestions will be accepted. Edith's recommendation of a little prayer is good, whatever the religious belief of the dying person. If the one dying has never had a religion, that is no hindrance. The quiet sincere offering of a wish for the peace and welfare of the dying one is the spiritual equivalent of a prayer because the motive is the same.

Boerstler suggests merely breathing in time with the patient's breathing, in a simple process that he calls just "Letting Go." The presence of a quiet, calm friend or hospice helper who will hold the dying one's hand and perhaps speak softly now and then is probably the most important function of the person who watches and assists at the bedside.

Understanding the actual changes during the transition processes is also a great comfort to the dying person. He or she does not feel that this is fearsome unfamiliar territory into which one is being forced but is a peaceful floating up out of the confining body or a dropping into a quiet, refreshing sleep, to waken free and strong.

To hospice workers and relatives I would say the same thing: Place yourself temporarily in the place of this dying person and ask yourself what you would like to have the people around you do or say as you relax and prepare to leave your body. You would want quietness rather than turmoil, soft words of love and tenderness rather than weeping and frantic calls to remain. Sweet old memories would be welcome. Assurance of forgiveness and soft requests to be forgiven would be of great comfort. Your own hearts will tell you what is needed. And then when the breathing ceases, let the quietness continue, quietness of the emotions of the watchers and relatives as well as quietness in the room. All is well. Let the dying person's consciousness vacate the body completely and feel the joy, the lightness, the freedom that Edith described with such bubbling effervescent laughter!

Self Controlled Transition

Self-assisted or self-controlled death, called "conscious dying," has been known and practiced among some of the

Eastern mystics for a very long time. Some American Indians also have been acquainted with the methods by which a person may choose a time and let the body die.

Although I had heard of such methods, the first I encountered personally was in 1981 in a class I was teaching on Regression Hypnosis. Jokingly I had suggested to my students that they select one among themselves "to die for us next time," meaning to regress to a death in a past life. At the next class session I asked if anyone had volunteered to die today. Vickie raised her hand at once.

"We were talking about that on the ride here this morning," she said. "I'd like to go back to when I was an Indian. I've been having flash-backs to a buffalo stampede."

My wording to Vickie when she was in hypnosis was, "Let your mind take us to a time in a past life when you had an easy, pleasant death experience." (Afterward Vickie told us that when she first entered the altered state she saw again the buffalo herd stampeding, but at my words "an easy, pleasant death experience" the buffalo herd disappeared and she found herself in a different location.)

In brief, this is what Vickie reported:

> "I am an old man, an Indian shaman. It is time for me to leave. I have been living with my two wives in a hogan a little distance from the village.
>
> "My people respect me and depend upon me to protect them. My wives, too, are medicine people. They know without words what is in my mind to do, and they are willing; they understand.
>
> "I fast for three days. Then I leave my house taking very little with me, for I shall need little. I walk; I climb; I go to the top of the sacred mountain, and there on a flat rock I stand and pray to the four directions."
>
> There was a pause, then the voice said, "The old man is lying down. ... I see the old man lying there, face up toward the sky. He has left his body."

I interrupted quietly as the facilitator, wishing to contact more about the actual transition processes for the sake of the students: "Return to the moment when the old man finishes his prayer, and continue from there, getting all the details."

Again there was a pause. . . "The old man is lying down. . . . He has left his body."

Several times Vickie relived the transition, each time as simply as the first time. There seemed to be no interval, no intervening processes, just a rising up of the consciousness and looking down at the body.

The people of the tribe believed that the spirit of one dead might remain close and harm them if they stayed in the same location. Therefore the custom was for the entire tribe to move to another place after the death of an important person. I asked the shaman about this custom.

"They need not fear me. I would not hurt them. They are my people; I protect them. They will turn now to my wives for help and protection, and after them, to a child soon to be born who will grow to be their next shaman."

I did not ask whether the child to be born was one of his own children. We received the clear impression that genetic descent was of less importance than spiritual preparedness.

(Years later Vickie wrote me that on a trip with her family through the Dakotas she had recognized that certain mountain and had even made out the very ledge where the old man had laid his body down.)

A rather similar case of self-performed transition by another Indian shaman was contacted when a man, a member of our meditation group, regressed to a death experience in a past life as a woman. The elderly medicine woman walked alone out of the village to an isolated place near the edge of a cliff overlooking the ocean. There she lay down, arranged her garments, and apparently "disassembled the atoms" of her body (vaporized it?) leaving the empty garments on the ground, presumably for her people to find later.

With assisted and self-controlled transitions most of the thinking and planning has been done before the final act. The final act itself may be less important in the spiritual sense than the foregoing thoughts and emotions. Because the decisions have already been made, the mind of the person is usually at ease, even though the external circumstances may be far from peaceful. The mind of the one dying may actually be able to choose to remain in painful or distressing circumstances or to vacate the body more quickly than might be expected.

An amazingly self-controlled example is that of Quang Duc's death in Saigon in 1963. A Buddhist monk from the age of fifteen, he was now sixty-six when he decided to offer his life as a sacrificial protest against the terrible war in Viet Nam. Two other monks were like-minded, but because of his seniority it was he who had himself driven to a crowded street corner in Saigon on the morning of June 11, 1963, and, sitting cross-legged on the pavement, had some of his disciples drench him with gasoline and set him afire.

Reported by Malcolm Browne of the Associated Press (who had been tipped off by Buddhist militants and was waiting with a camera) and described by Stanley Karnow in his book, *Viet Nam: A History*, the elderly monk sat perfectly still and

> pressed his palms together in prayer as a sheet of flame the color of his orange robe enveloped him. Pedestrians, amazed by the awesome sight, prostrated themselves in reverence, and even a nearby policeman threw himself to the ground. Trucks and automobiles stopped, snarling traffic. By the time an ambulance arrived, the old man had fallen over, still burning as the fire consumed his flesh. Only his heart remained intact.

(The militants) also handed reporters copies of a biography of the suicide. . . . The document included his last words, a "respectful" plea to (General) Diem to show "charity and compassion" to all religions.

A different type of self-controlled dying comes to mind, one reported and filmed in the 1970s by two British brothers, Lawrence and Lorne Blair. On the island of Bali they met an ancient man said to be well over one hundred years old, a famous Oriental artist, who planned so that each of his pictures was finished at a certain time of the year that he believed was astrologically the best time for completion.

Now, his body reduced by age to a mere skeleton topped by a smiling face—the smile almost toothless but the eyes bright—his fingernails grown long and claw-like—the ancient was waiting cheerfully for the time of completion to arrive again. This time he chose it to complete his life.

The British brothers talked with the old man, photographed him and many of his pictures, and took moving pictures of him and his family, and when they left, they promised to return. But they came back a few days too late to speak to him again. They were told that on the day selected, he called his family around him on the porch of his dwelling, spoke and said good-bye to each one, including all his great-grandchildren and other relatives, and then lay down and let his consciousness depart from the body.

The Blair brothers were allowed to photograph the old man's body as it was carried to the prepared burning place, looking almost as it had in life. His family showed no grief, for after all, he had a long, satisfying life in that body, and now it was the time of completion. (The film was shown on BBC and rerun in the U.S. on PBS.)

Another modern case of self-governed transition is that of an elderly woman whose unmarried daughter, a friend of mine, had been taking care of her for many years. As the mother became weaker and more helpless, the daughter seemed to cling ever more tightly to her.

Finally the mother began to urge, "Violet, Honey, let me go. Let me go."

The daughter could not release the mother psychologically even then—not until I spoke gently one day of the selfishness of forcing the mother to remain in her old ailing body, and the generosity that the act of release on the part of the daughter would be, freeing the mother from the pain and weariness.

Violet told me later, "I told Mother that if she wanted to go, I was letting her go. And a little while later when I went to her, she looked up at me with such a bright loving look, straight into my eyes. She was there—and then was gone. I know she was telling me good-bye. . . . And it's all right." Tears had come to Violet's eyes but she was composed.

And it *was* all right.

The Death of Buddha, 488 B.C.E. is a fine example of self-controlled transition. (The following is condensed and paraphrased from the Buddhist Scriptures in Pali)

> When the Buddha was eighty years old, he told his disciples that in three months he would die. Their reaction was what most people would have had: shock, denial, grief. For forty-five years since the momentous night of Enlightenment that had climaxed seven years of searching, suffering, and seeking answers, he had traversed the land on foot, teaching—teaching kings and outcastes alike. Now his body was tired, and the monks were well instructed and could carry on the Teachings.
>
> Three months later at a feast prepared for him and his monks by Chunda, a smith and a faithful lay disciple, the Master sensed that one of the dishes contained poison

mushrooms, unsuspected by the devoted host. Rather than distressing Chunda with this information, the Master called him and told him to serve the other monks with all the delicacies except this one, which he told Chunda could be assimilated only by a Tathagata such as he. Therefore this dish was to be for him alone; any portion remaining un-eaten was to be buried deeply.

After the feast was finished, knowing that his time was short, the Master led his disciples along the forest road toward the next city but was overcome with weakness at an ashram before reaching it, and asked his followers to pre-pare a place under twin sala trees for him to rest.

Some of them were mentally blaming their recent host for having given unclean food to the Master. But the Master was already aware of such a possible attitude and told them that in case Chunda should berate himself and be full of grief when learning of the Master's illness, Chunda was to be assured that he was blameless and was rather to feel honored, because the last meal given to an Enlightened One was one of the most sacred of the entire life.

His conscious mind was clear in spite of the mortal sickness and his thoughts were for his monks. He noted that his beloved cousin-disciple and personal body-servant, Ananda, was absent from the circle around him. Ananda was found leaning against the door of the ashram, weeping: "I am not yet perfected, and the Master is about to leave us—he who is so kind."

The Master sent for Ananda, comforted him and spoke, honoring him in the presence of all the monks. Then, after a few last words to the sorrowing disciples, reminding them, "Be ye lamps unto your own feet; work out your own salvation with diligence," he let his consciousness rise stage by stage to the highest level of contemplation, that Ninth Condition which he called "Neither Conscious nor Uncon-scious."

From that state he allowed his mind to drop back, stage by stage, to the level of the First Trance of meditation, then back up to the Fourth Trance, from which he left the body. The disciples in reverent silence followed the course of the Master's mind as his mind moved through the levels of meditation and contemplation under full control, and then entered the blessed freedom of Nirvana.

During the days and weeks after the burning, the monks still mourned what they perceived as their great loss—all but the Arhants, the saints, among whom was an elderly monk who went about with an attitude of joyfulness. When a younger monk inquired as to how he could keep so cheery a mien when the Master was gone, the elder replied, "I feel him with me every moment." And in that instant he beheld the Master in a shining vision! The story of his vision spread swiftly through the company of the monks, and those who had felt desolate were now comforted.

A Contemporary Self-assisted Transition

On November 2, 1997, Kathleen Majka, R.N., told our class on Transition the story of her friend, "Nellie," who had just died.

Nellie, 85, was living alone near Cortez, Colorado, her husband having died a few years before. The lady was becoming unable to cook for herself, to start the propane heater, etc., so her children were urging her to move in with one of them. But she was stubbornly insisting, "My husband died in *that bed*, and I'm going to die in *that bed*."

When the children asked the priest, Father McGuinness, to go and give her the Last Rites (which now are often offered as a healing modality, not merely as the Last Sacrament), she laughed and told him, "I'm not ready yet." However, she accepted the Sacrament.

Some time later she began having trouble with her kidneys and had to go to the hospital. This time when the priest visited her she told him, "I'm ready now. How do I do it?"

"Just say three times to Jesus, 'I commend my soul to thee,'" said Father McGuinness. The elderly parish priest had dealt with the dying often and took her question as matter-of-factly as she had asked it.

After going home Nellie invited her whole family—brother and sister from Denver, all her children and grand-children—to come for a reunion. (Kathleen was not sure whether she told them what she had in mind.) When all were there, Nellie told herself the words on a Monday evening in mid-October, 1997. Nothing happened. She said them again on Tuesday, Wednesday, Thursday, and by Friday must have been adding what the priest had also suggested, "and hurry up, please."

Then during that good day with her family she retired for a nap . . . and her body did not wake up. She had passed peacefully during sleep, in "that bed."

Later Kathleen wrote, adding more details:

"Nellie was very pragmatic. Her failing health made her decide not to live through another snow, because the lane to her house was a quarter of a mile long, and also she didn't want to spend the money for a cord of wood for the winter. She decided to die, preferably on her deceased husband's birthday.

"I'd been visiting her daily for more than two years and was planning a camping trip in Arizona around the time of her husband's birthday. Since her primary care-giver (me) was leaving, she could ask the children to come and help her out without their suspecting. It was fascinating to watch the joy with which she planned her death.

"The day I left she took to her deathbed. She asked her children to call Denver and get her sister, 81, and the rest of the family. (I think one daughter-in-law was privy to the plan but the rest didn't know she had 'commended her soul.')

"She had a great time seeing everyone and knowing who would be at her funeral. It was like holding court. The whole affair was planned around good travel conditions and clement weather for her family. She wanted everyone who could come to be there. I think that is why she held out for five days. She was lucid and planning until the end.

"I know all of this because I called five days after deathbed day 1. She told me how wonderful it was, and said she was glad I had called so she could say she loved me, and thank you, and good-bye. She missed her husband's birthday, but died the day after I spoke with her. She really did enjoy her last days!"

4

IMMEDIATE CAUSES
OF DEATH

BY "IMMEDIATE CAUSES" OF DEATH I mean the physical causes,
ignoring for the present the spiritual/social causes. Physical
causes may be either sudden, as in accidents or battle, or
quiet, from natural causes, e.g., senility or degenerative conditions—or from fatal diseases or the weakened condition
following accidents.

Quiet Death

When the person has had a deteriorating condition for a
while, both the person and his/her relatives and friends may
have had time to think of the possibility of death and be a
little prepared for any change to come. When the patient's
body does cease to function, therefore, there is somewhat
less emotional and mental shock for the survivors.

This is not to say that the days or months before the hour
of death are usually easy for either the patient or the relatives
and care-givers. The weeks and months may drag out far
longer than anyone would desire. When the final moments
do arrive, however, the passing is usually quiet and easy.

63

My father began to show symptoms of an undiagnosed condition when he was about sixty. It resembled Lateral Sclerosis (Lou Gehrig's Disease) but was atypical and had begun much later in life than in most such cases. My mother's death seemed to hasten the process; he lost successively his strength, ambition, and sense of balance, his former sense of humor, and finally the power of speech while always remaining quiet and cooperative, and outwardly cheerful. Tests suggested no helpful type of treatment. After being bedfast for more than five months, his time finally came. He became comatose, breathing rapidly while his temperature soared. I was beside him, bathing his head and chest, when the breathing suddenly became much slower and more shallow and then simply stopped. I laid my hand on his chest; his heart was still beating, but it ceased in a minute or two. There was no struggle at all.

I regret that I did not know at that time that his mind, freed from the confines of his old body, was probably right there still and could have heard me if I had spoken to him. I hope that he heard my thoughts, but I did not speak aloud. At least he did have quietness during his passing and was not the center of a turmoil of tubes and needles, voices and hurrying feet.

Another passing just as simple was a past-life death of a friend and coworker, Bernice Garber, LSW II. She writes of it in 1994:

> I was a very old man with a long white beard, living in olden times—about 1600–1700. I lived in the country with my wife (who was rather irritable, dependent, and demanding). I worked hard—a farmer—and was well liked in the village.
>
> One day I felt tired. It was a beautiful day and I walked to my favorite place—a big tree in the field that provided a

lot of shade. I sat down under it and fell asleep—and died. It was quiet and peaceful.

Some time after dying I returned to my home to see how my wife would be. She was very upset, but I knew she could take care of herself and would be all right.

I went to the Light, then, I think.

One more example of a quiet passing I quote from Lord Hugh Dowding's book, *Lychgate: The Entrance to the Path* (1945), in which he wrote about the "Rescue Work" that he and a London group were doing to assist the confused earthbound souls of soldiers killed in World War II. One was an Irish soldier, who at first went with the (discarnate) guide who came to help him, but then "was called home by thoughts so insistent that I had to go."

It was wee Mary, our youngest, only two years old, and she got sick with pneumonia and the wife prayed and prayed, but it didn't do any good. I sat by her side, the wee one, she was so bad, I could feel her little hand all hot and feverish, and then suddenly she looked up and saw me, and climbed out of her cot into my arms, just like she used to do, and I held her for ever so long in great happiness, and then I thought maybe I'd best put her into her cot again, and as I went to do it I saw she was in bed lying so quiet and still, and a child just like her was in my arms, and as I turned, uncertain what to do, a beautiful lady came and said to me, "Take her with you, no need to stay in the house now, take her into the sunshine, she is yours now and for always, and she will be your special care."

So I took her out and we sat on the hillside, and played with flowers and pebbles, and when I'd left her asleep out there I went back into the house. I found only grief and mourning . . . and then I knew that wee Mary had come to join me . . . and I understood that death wasn't real, but Life everlasting was TRUE, TRUE, TRUE. . . ."

These three examples are of peaceful, quiet deaths, one in the first person by the one who died (the old man); one in third person, by the one watching and attending (my father's death); and one related by the already deceased father who watched and assisted (wee Mary). Many other instances might be given here, and some are scattered throughout the book under other headings. All of them have the same qualities of ease and simplicity, and give a sense of being a natural process.

Sudden Death

Abrupt termination of the body's life need not be from violent causes. Stroke (apoplexy) and cardiac arrest may cause sudden death and may even be considered "natural" causes.

Many sudden deaths are by violent means, however: e.g., murder (including death by abuse), suicide (which is self-murder), fatal wounds in battle, or even, in modern warfare, the abrupt disintegration of the whole body by explosion or vaporization. Accidents often cause sudden death as well. In this class might be included accidental deaths from natural disasters such as floods, earthquakes, volcanic eruptions, hurricanes, tornadoes, mudslides, and wildfires, although sometimes the dying is less instantaneous than in other cases.

A number of my friends say that they would like to die suddenly rather than more slowly. They have in mind the long drawn out lingering that occurs in chronic diseases before the person can die. Actually, however, a somewhat slower death is often easier than an abrupt one. It is somewhat like the difference between drifting into sleep or being whacked into unconsciousness.

Many deaths are natural in the course of Nature, not only in the Animal Kingdom but in the Human Kingdom as well. Some persons killed abruptly may experience something like an electric shock and find the consciousness floating and the thoughts momentarily confused, bewildered, or dazed. Others may find the consciousness leaves the body before the body succumbs.

When I first read of such a case as the latter, in which the consciousness left the person's body before the body sank and drowned, it was merely another bit of an incredible anecdote to be put aside for future consideration when, if ever, I had more information. Since then I have encountered other cases in my own practice. The two illustrations here are from past-life regressions:

My client went back to a life as an Indian man who lived on the top of a high mesa. The trail up to the village was almost vertical, but well worn from constant use. On this day the man was ascending the familiar steep path when a stone loosened under his foot and he lost his grip.

He knew instantly what had happened and what the result of the long vertical fall would be. He saw something falling from the face of the cliff—a human body—and then realized that it was his body. There was no panic, no fear, only an interested observation.

In the second case the subject was not a client but a friend of one of my sons, visiting from New Zealand. Interested in regressions and past lives, he went back in hypnosis to a previous time when, again as a young man and again an experienced climber and explorer as now, he saw himself fall when the ice-cliff he was climbing shelled off some ice under his feet. Calmly he reported seeing his body fall, saw it crumpled at the base of the ice cliff, saw his companions rush to it, lift it onto a hurriedly made litter, and carry it away.

"Where are *you?*" I asked.

"About thirty feet above and a little behind," he said. "I'm floating along."

"You are just a young man, strong and healthy. Do you want to get back into your body?"

"Mmmm . . . I'm peaceful," was his answer.

Such an emotional attitude of tranquillity is the usual feeling after the body has been vacated.

A more recent accident, involving present-life deaths, was that which occurred in Amsterdam, Holland, when a large airplane went out of control and crashed into an apartment building in the night, killing all of the passengers and crew and many persons sleeping in the apartments. At the end of a workshop that a friend and I were giving in California in 1992, a woman in the audience asked if we could contact the souls of those killed in Amsterdam and assist them in some way. With only a few minutes of our time remaining I was hesitant, but when I asked the channel's Higher Mind whether we should try to contact these souls, the answer from Mary's Higher Mind and relayed through her finger-movement, said, "Yes."

Therefore, in the ten minutes or so of our remaining time, I asked first for a spokesperson from among the plane's crew to come and talk to us. The pilot of the plane came. He was the only member of the entire group of people on the plane who was still earth-bound. He alone had ridden the plane clear to the moment of impact. The channel said that all the other crew members and all of the passengers had left their bodies before that moment and had gone on—in other words, they were all "dead" before their bodies died, probably because they had a few moments of forewarning. But "the captain went down with his ship."

After assisting the pilot to let go his guilt and fear and go safely into the Light, I asked for a spokesperson from among the people in the apartments who had been killed. Mary, the channel, saw a young woman come. She said her name was Linda. (To myself I wondered about the name: For a Hollander? A Dutch woman? Later someone told me that "Linda" is not uncommon among the Dutch.)

Linda said that many of the victims were still in a state of shock, numb and dazed from the abruptness of the change. They were, I believe, much like victims of a car accident who, when knocked unconscious, might awaken later, stare around at white walls, look up and see a nurse, and ask, "What happened? Where am I?"

I explained to Linda what had happened and asked her to relay the information to the rest and ask them to contact their survivors to comfort and reassure them. She was uncertain as to whether she could spread the information to all of them. So we, as a group in California, meditated and sent thoughts of consolation and reassurance to both the souls of those killed and to their surviving families.

The "success" of such meditations is not capable of being "proved," of course, by any modern means. Nevertheless it seems sensible to many of us who meditate to adopt as a motto in such cases, *"It can't hurt and may help."* Mary, the channel in hypnosis, told us that she saw Linda and heard her thoughts (in English, although Linda was probably thinking in Dutch), and perceived many in the group of stunned, dazed souls gradually awakening and following a Guide into the Light.

Death by Violence

In cases of murder the victim may feel intense fear and from the moments of dying carry the emotion into the next state and into the next life. The first reaction after death may be a desire to get away and find a safe place in which to hide (as murder victims, children killed by abuse, and aborted infants usually do), or else, filled with rage, to stay near the attacker and try to get revenge.

A beautiful, talented young woman came to me after becoming disenchanted with her former therapist. She told me that a neighbor had reported to the police that she and her husband were concealing hard drugs in their home. When the police came to her door, she went into a state of total panic as soon as she saw their uniforms. She could not speak except to gasp out that the three marijuana plants were for personal use, not to sell, and they had no hard drugs at all. When asked to sign something, she could not read the paper and could not write even her name. (Much of this reaction was due to the fact that her policeman father had routinely beaten her and her brother as children, telling them that policemen never beat anyone who wasn't bad. Some of the beatings were so severe that permanent scars were left. Nor could she trust anyone, her therapist, her lawyer, or even her husband, a good deal of the time)

Regressed first to the recent experience, then to the childhood experiences, and finally to a past life, we learned that in the 1920s she had been a very attractive dancer in a town of fair size and had been invited to "go some place" with one of the nicely dressed young men who had watched her dance. She liked him, so she agreed, but when he took her to a deserted place, she began to scream. In his anger at the noise, he stabbed her to death, "but my mouth was still screaming—it stayed open," she said.

Her body was not found immediately but was taken away eventually and buried as she watched from a distance, feeling sad that no one knew her well enough to be her friend and to attend the burial. In the regression she identified one of the policemen who had terrified her in this life as the man who killed her in the past life. In both experiences there was the strong feeling of aloneness and helplessness, with no one to care about or protect her.

This young lady had definite symptoms of paranoia, partly due to another past life. She terminated therapy after getting this much, although I felt that there was considerably more that needed to be neutralized. I heard from some of her acquaintances that her symptoms were still in evidence. Then she moved away and I lost track of her. I consider this one of the times when I failed in therapy.

In a case of *suicide* the person, old or young, may have been feeling unloved, useless, in total despair. The fatal act may require the person to work up his or her courage or it may be an impulsive act performed almost without thought. In many cases the person so deep in despair is probably not thinking of the effect his suicide may have on others, unless he is holding the thought, "They'll be sorry when I'm no longer here."

I know several cases of deliberate, selfless suicide, in which the person carefully considered all the various factors and came up with the conclusion that his death would be the best in the long run for everyone. One was a man who had been a classmate of mine in high school. When he learned in middle-age that his cancer was incurable, he took his life, I was told, in order that his family could have his insurance and not be overwhelmed by the expenses of a long period of useless treatment for him, nor would he have to endure that long period of increasing helplessness and pain.

Another instance was that of an American soldier in Korea, married to a Korean woman. When he was discharged to come back to the States, he was told he could not bring his wife and little girl with him. Nor could he send for them later. His final decision, doubtless made after intense and agonizing inward debate, was to kill himself so that his wife, as a widow of an American soldier, and his child could have veteran's benefits from his service. His suicide was from a purely unselfish motive. The motive was good, but the result was not as good as he would have liked. The American man his widow married, the man who brought her and the child to the U.S., had an embittered mother who never accepted the Korean wife, and in her own loneliness, the wife failed to see that the little girl was as lonely as she herself was. Nor did the new American father seem to understand all this. There has been some adjustment for the wife, but now she is worried and unhappy about the girl's teenage rebelliousness. It must be a sadness to the deceased father to perceive how his ultimate self-sacrifice has failed to achieve all the happiness and acceptance for his wife that he had hoped for. Even when the motive is pure, the result may not be entirely good.

Most suicides, however, are trying to escape from their personal problems, pains, frustrations, and loneliness of the present life and to find peace and quietness. All this is understandable, but the suicidal person lacks knowledge of the law of Karma and also of the facts about death.

Suicide is self murder, the destruction of a wonderful body meant to serve as a means of learning various spiritual lessons during earth-existence. Some of the lessons are very hard, it is true; some seem very cruel. The act of self-murder, however, is rarely a good way to deal with even terrible problems, which in most cases will have to be faced in a future life if not dealt with in the present. Suicide may seem to be the easy way out. It may take greater courage to stay and face life's challenges and trials than to take "the easy way out." *Every suicidal person has need of assistance and support* from friends or professionals. Sometimes life's troubles are too heavy for one person to bear alone. Suicide does not solve the problems nor relieve the troubles, however.

One of my young friends, "Cindy," a lovely intelligent young woman with a keen eye for beauty, found herself in circumstances that sent her into depression and finally despair. Friends did try to help her, but life circumstances could not easily be changed. When her husband was out of town, she killed herself. When her husband returned he found her body.

I felt that Cindy was still in trouble. With a co-worker as channel, I called Cindy to come and talk with me. In a few moments her voice, colorless and flat, said through the channel, "Hello, Mother Louise."

"Are you all right?" I asked.

"No," she answered in the same dead voice.

In response to my questions she said, "I just couldn't stand the pain any more." (She meant emotional pain.) "But I don't think this helped; in fact, in some ways it's worse. All there is to do is sit and think."

She began to drift off. My questions received no answers; there was an empty silence. I called her back urgently, not wanting her to disappear into the mist of mental dimness and guilt.

When I asked for someone who cared about her to come to help her, she said she saw her grandfather coming. As I felt that he would be able to give her the comfort and encouragement that she needed, I terminated the contact, resolving to check up on her at a future time.

The next contact was several months later. This time Cindy's voice contained more life, though she was still depressed. She admitted that her grandfather was "available" but did not indicate that she let him help her much, if at all. She said she had a teacher but did not sound as if she cared. She was still deep in feelings of guilt and remorse.

I asked the teacher to please come. Using my position as both therapist and friend to Cindy, I told the teacher, a woman, that I felt perhaps Cindy was being—ah—perhaps stubborn, or—ah—(I sought for a better word, but the teacher interrupted dryly, "That word will do.")

Programming Cindy to look for light in her dark surroundings, to be receptive to her teacher, and to allow her grandfather to help her, I left her this time able to see at least the glow as of a sunrise and feel warmth in the former chill.

Not until my co-worker, Mary, and I were giving a workshop on Rescue Work in 1992 did I try to contact Cindy again. Then, asking each member of my audience to select and call a friend or relative who had committed suicide and speak or murmur the name aloud, I, too, spoke a name: "Cindy, I am calling you. You were not ready before, but now it is time. Please come." Then I asked for a guide to come for each soul, or for the group as a whole.

Afterward Mary, the channel, told us, "Most of the souls were just a group, rather dim and featureless to me, but one woman—young, I think—came and was right here beside me. I felt I could have touched her. She had long hair in a ponytail. I could not see her face. She was the very last to go."

I think that young long-haired woman was Cindy. It was an intuitive feeling, and my response was an emotional sense of great relief and happiness for her.

I mentioned earlier that Mary felt the gratitude of the souls we had assisted. "It was almost overwhelming," she added. "They thought everyone had forgotten them."

Executions are usually forms of sudden violent death. Our group has had a few cases in which the executed person was contacted after death through a channel.

In one case the electrocuted man felt that he was still confined in a cell with no window except a barred skylight far above him. There he sat, passively accepting his fate, not aware that he was now dead nor that his thoughts and desires could sweep away the bars from the skylights and that his desires could also let him float up to freedom. His feelings of guilt in this case held him down. We helped him to "clean up" his feelings of anger, frustration, unworthiness, and fear, to understand how he had injured other people, and at last to see the Light and accept the assistance of the guide who came for him.

In another case, after his summary execution by a police officer's bullet at the scene of the crime, the criminal escaped at once, leaving his body and roaming freely among living people, pausing to influence or even invade one or another as the mood of the *victim* permitted. His own mood was one of rage, bitterness, and arrogant insensitivity. We contacted him during a meeting of our meditation group. When we conversed with him through Lanetta as channel, he claimed to be Huberty, the man who had shot up the McDonald's in California. He said that before this life he was Hitler's young nephew killed at the age of ten by an Allied bomb. He was as full of childish hate for Americans as he was full of admiration for Hitler. "He can kill as many people as he wants," he boasted.

This soul was not interested in cleaning himself up nor in trying to discern a Light. His rage did gradually diminish as we talked with him, and he asked to remain in the room with us. Lanetta, the retired Army nurse, ordered him over to the far side of the room, and I added that he might listen but not bother nor influence us in any way. Lanetta told us afterward that he obeyed, listening, perplexed, to us as we worked to help other wandering or lost souls, "as if he had never been with people like us before and could not understand," she said.

With her permission he came back to her house the following day and occupied her porch swing, which once again, as on the previous visit, began to swing with no visible person in it, and no wind to move it. To her question he indicated that he was still not interested in moving into the Light but was not here to harm her. So far as any of us know, he is still at large but at least has some new things to think about. He has free will, as does every soul, and we do not coerce, although we do urge with as much gentle, firm, persuasive power as possible. Some of our persuasion was to direct his attention to the law of Karma, that whatever one does to others comes back to one's self sooner or later.

In any case, the psyche of an executed condemned person still lives. Our impression is that seldom does an execution result in anything but the release of the executed person's psyche, which may remain earth-bound for an indefinite time. Even if the executed person was innocent, he may still be burdened with anger, fear, feelings of futility and helplessness. If the criminal was guilty there may be these as well as rage and guilt. But the Light comes for every soul. In reality it is always there, but it cannot be seen nor felt until the soul is open and receptive and has put off the heaviest of the old feelings. Over and over we find that there is *always the opportunity for the soul to have another chance* to be sorry, to ask forgiveness, to receive help when the soul is willing. We are told by the Spiritual Advisors, "What is important is the message of *the beauty of Death. Even a dark life still has forgiveness.*"

Accidents

There are so many different kinds of accidents that a few illustrative cases will have to suffice. Accidental deaths vary from trivial causes to great tragedies.

In a past-life regression one of my female clients went back to a life in which she was a teenaged girl in Colonial times. She could not resist dressing in her new full-skirted party gown and party shoes and running outside to show her family. Crossing the rushing creek, she slipped on one of the stepping stones—and abruptly saw, from a position above, "a flower going down the river . . ."—a flower which she semiconsciously knew was her body surrounded by the billowing skirt of her precious colorful gown. She felt she must follow the flower. . . . She was held earthbound by her admiration and attraction for the gown and her body. We had to help her to let go of these emotional attachments before she could move on away from the earthbound condition.

Before the *Challenger* space craft went up in January, 1986, one of the ladies in our group felt strongly that its stuck door should remain closed and not be opened to let the flight preparations be completed. When the door was finally opened, when the crew was inside, when the countdown began, Ruth sat with her eyes on the television, still mentally urging that the flight be canceled even at this last moment.

It wasn't. Ruth watched what she knew was going to happen: the explosion. Instantly, being prepared, she sent out a strong mental call for the crew to come to her home. They came, and Ruth, though not seeing them, was able to hear them and feel their vibrations.

She explained to them what had happened. She told us later that one man hung back—the pilot or navigator, she thought. Christa, the teacher, quickly understood that they were all now "dead," as did the one black man. When the other woman of the crew, an engineer, finally did accept that now they would "go on," Ruth said the engineer grasped her notebook and pen (of astral substance now), ready to take notes on the new situation, but Christa gently plucked them out of her hands, saying, "You won't need these where we are going." Ruth had the clear impression that Christa had suggested before the lift-off that they pray together, and they had prayed the Lord's prayer. (We recall that "Deliver us from evil" does not necessarily mean from death.)

Later, in the meditation group, we called the crew of the Challenger again. We asked them how they had found Ruth's house when she called them.

"We didn't know what had happened—we were confused—but then we saw something in the distance like a big orange-colored flower, like a great calla lily glowing in the grayness, and we came to it." (Clairvoyants might have described it as a thought-form created by Ruth's mental call.)

Christa and the officer who hung back were not ready to go on, the latter because of his still-unresolved skepticism, the former because, "I want to go home and experience my family."

I agreed that she could do that, but warned her not to go too close to any of the members nor to stay too long, lest the magnetic pull of their living physical bodies or the drawing of their emotions might draw her in as an obsessing entity so that she could not escape.

When the rest of the crew finally departed, however, both Christa and the officer went with the others. We reminded them that they could send their thoughts of love and consolation to their families and friends, and hope that the families would be open and receptive to them.

Deaths in War

Battles of all historic and prehistoric ages account for multitudes of earthbound psyches because a death in battle—whether sudden or slower and more painful—is accompanied by numerous strong negative feelings both physical and emotional. Perhaps death as the result of a fight between two individuals might be considered "natural," inasmuch as it occurs frequently in nature. Even a duel contains strong harsh emotions. But wholesale killing for political, ethnic, or religious reasons is certainly unnatural.

There is a great difference between these mass deaths in wars and the mass deaths from natural causes—floods, hurricanes, earthquakes, and so on. In war powerful feelings of rage, hate, and viciousness take over the personalities of many persons, both soldiers and civilians, these emotions based usually on fear and cultivated hate but also inculcated into the very psyche of the warriors by their training.

In natural disasters and accidents, on the other hand, the intense emotions, although at first based on fear and self-preservation, turn quickly to thoughts of preserving the lives of others, of helping one another both during and after the climax of the disaster. Many souls rise naturally into the next dimension when losing the body. It is true that many souls do remain earth-bound after natural disasters, but the composition of their emotions is such that they are easily helped to understand their situation as being "dead" and to move on into the next dimension.

Many soldiers, sailors, and flyers killed in war also quickly understand, of course, when contacted by the living in hypnosis or in meditation. Such contacts by the living, with the purpose of assisting the lost earth-bound souls, has been called "Rescue Work."

During and after World War II, Lord Dowding, then Chief Marshall of the Royal Air Force, and a group of psychics and meditators in London worked to assist the deceased men who came or were brought by discarnate co-workers to the group. Case after case is reported in some detail in Dowding's book. Most of the rescued souls were British, a number were Americans, and there were even a few Germans. Some civilians were also contacted.

A couple of examples follow. The first is from a young British sailor:

"My name's Cox. I was a gunner, and oh she was a beauty" (patting a gun). "Can I say how many planes she brought down?" His gun got 15 Jerries. . . .

"They won't find no body for me, because we got it fair and square. The Padre here tells me I was blown up. I didn't know about that. All I know is that one minute we were blasting away and all Hell was let loose, a noisy Hell, and then it seemed that the next minute I was in the most beautiful and peaceful garden. Just think of it! One minute reek and smoke, and noise indescribable, and the next, clear sunshine, green grass, and the birds singing.

"I was a bit surprised like, and thought I was dreaming. . . .

"Suddenly I found myself asking the Padre where we were. The place was familiar, yet not familiar. His answer fair blew me down the hatch, because he said, 'You are in your own home, one you built for yourself while you were still living on the Earth.' That took some swallowing! But he explained it so naturally, reminding me of the battle. . . ."

The second account quoted was told by a British civilian:

No, I'm not a soldier, only a munitions maker. I was done in, in the last London raid. I was underground and the floor gave way, and all the machinery on top came down onto us; it was an awful show, I screamed when I saw it coming. The fire broke out before anyone could stop it, and I saw it coming towards me—fire and tangled parts of machinery and molten metal; there wasn't a chance of escaping for any of us. The pain didn't last very long, but much longer than our bodies. I kept on feeling it whenever I looked at my body, and I couldn't leave it somehow until Jane came. Jane is a girl who worked near me; she came and took my arm and led me away. . . . (Jane, of course, was killed at the same time.)

After the suicide-bombing of the barracks in Beirut (October 23, 1993) which killed about two hundred American soldiers, our meditation group contacted a few of those killed. One young soldier, finding himself still alive in a gray expanse, said, "They didn't tell us it would be like this." Poor fellow—"they" didn't tell him because "they" didn't know themselves, and would not have believed even if they had been told! Can you imagine a Master Sergeant—?

When we contacted those soldiers in Beirut, we were told that of the entire number there was only one man who was really prepared for death: a young Hispanic man whose mother had reminded him before he left the United States that if, being a soldier, he were to get killed, he might have a moment of confusion after death, wondering what had happened, but soon he would realize the situation and would know that he was to go on to the next world. Her son remembered her words and took the great change calmly, after that first moment of confusion.

It is possible that other mothers, fathers, wives, or friends had mentioned the possibility of dying to their soldier-loved ones, too, but if so, the soldiers passed their reminders from their memories or felt that only the other fellows might die.

Death to a Muslim can mean almost opposite things. To a soldier who dies in battle or is killed by a bomb or other military means, death is a spiritual honor and the soul goes at once to a bright world of spirit. Except when it occurs in defense of their country or their religion, however, death can be another matter.

During the recent Gulf War a large group of women and children in Baghdad was killed when bombers mistook an air-raid shelter for a military target. When we contacted this group, the spokesperson who answered first, a young woman, said that they did not know where to go, for they were not worthy to go to a paradise. "This was a death without honor," she told us. "Our deaths were useless; they served no purpose."

After listening to our expressions of sorrow, our assurances about the love that Allah has for *all* his children and his desire that *all* be safe and comforted, she agreed to transmit our information to her fellow Muslims.

When some were ready to go on, she remarked, "The babies are still crying." Rather than speaking to the babies herself, she asked us to tell the babies that they would be carried safely to where "there is no more pain, no more fear." She declined our suggestion that she lead the group of those ready to go to the next level, saying, "I will stay here and help those who are not ready to go."

Such unselfishness is not common. Ani, this young Muslim woman without formal education, was of high intelligence and true spirituality.

As I ended this session, she—like a man in the group of Muslim pilgrims killed in the tunnel collapse (p. 102)—asked that the blessing of Allah be upon us for our assistance. I had told them both that the channel and I were "not of your religion but we wish to help." They accepted the help gratefully.

5

The Normal Pathways in the Next World

Immediately After Death

So now we are dead, by one means or another. Immediately after breath has ceased and the heart stopped beating, we remain nearby for a short time. (These are earth-terms, *nearby* and *short time*.) Usually we are just as much aware of ourselves and our surroundings as we were before separating from the body.

If the circumstances were more or less ordinary and quiet, we remain focused on the persons near the body, understanding all that they say, seeing all that they do, even perceiving what they are thinking. We may try to comfort the ones who are weeping, but we seem unable to make them hear. If we try to contact them by touch, our hand seems to go right through the physical substance of their arm or shoulder.

Some of us have even stayed until our funeral and attended our own services—feeling pleased, grieved, or irritated (as the case may be) by the words and thoughts of our friends and relatives and the officiating clergy!

We do not suddenly find ourselves pure, angelic, and perfected by the simple, natural ritual of dying. We retain all our human characteristics, both good and not-good. Former habits, thoughts, memories, attitudes, likes and dislikes—all these go with us as we leave the body and are preserved in these after-death stages as a unit, still as our "persona," our own *personality* identifiable by surviving friends and relatives in many large and small ways during conversations between us, the deceased, and the living, whether in a hypnotic session or in a Spiritualist meeting, or even by good fortune spontaneously.

If we were extremely ill or tired to exhaustion as we died, then after separation from the body we may *sleep for a time*, wakening later free of disease and weariness. Usually there is also relief from pain when we waken, or even right after leaving the body. In those of us who have had long-term diseases with various symptoms, however, the symptoms may hang over into this stage as if by mental habit: we *expect* to have continuing pain, fatigue, fear, or limitation. The *expectation* faithfully produces what we *expect* in this new world.

Similarly, if we have expected to find death as a long sleep or as complete oblivion or even total annihilation, we may prolong the *sleep state* after leaving the body. This is unfortunate and unnecessary. For those who sleep, there is a stagnation of activity and a cessation of spiritual and mental progress until they can be roused to take part in the beauty and activity of the non-physical worlds.

If as we died we were full of drugs, either prescribed or not, or were under the influence of alcohol or anesthetics, the effects of those may still be with us, confusing our mind as we leave the body and making our thought-processes slow and uncertain. If a friend or therapist suspects such a situation, it is a great help in clearing away these after-effects from our minds if someone will pray or if a therapist will say, "Let the mind of this one become clearer with each hour, each minute, that goes by. Let the effects of the drugs (alcohol, anesthetic) be totally neutralized, totally canceled, and this one's mind be clear again."

If the circumstances of dying were violent or painful, we may flee *away from the body* or from the distressing circumstances, seeking a different or safe place There may be changes in the environment as we do so. Cox, the Navy gunner, for example, found himself suddenly in a lovely peaceful meadow after his body was destroyed by a direct hit on his ship. The little girl who was left alone to die in the hot sun found herself under a cool starry sky, free to rise up and away from the flies, the burning sun, and the fears.

This *withdrawal from the earth-scene* is normally the next step. To us who have died, this "withdrawal' is more like a fading of the earth-scene. We say, "Things in the room seem to be getting dimmer; the people begin to look more ghostly to me now." We sometimes have a sense of being pulled up or whisked away, as the little girl was, but sometimes we seem to be pulled through a tunnel, which some of us have felt was dark and lonely, although others of us have sensed other souls there, but all describing a light at the end of the tunnel. Others of us do not see nor sense a tunnel. Some of us have not even sensed movement of any sort, just a sudden but smooth change in the environment from the heavy earth-plane to a lighter, brighter "place," as Edith Cox did.

Next Stages on the Normal Pathways

The next perception is usually of a *Light*, whether at the end of a tunnel or as a small dim light far away (by those whose lives have been clouded by negative feelings or doubts) but felt and seen by many as bright and warm, or even "all around." When we perceive the Light we feel an impulse to move toward it; we feel that it wants us, that it invites us to come. Some of us have sensed that it speaks and says, "Welcome." or "Come." One soul said, listening to the Light, "It sings!" The Light is felt—by almost all of us who have contemplated it—as being alive, intelligent, and loving: a *Being* of light.

And then, in or near the Light, we see a figure coming toward us: our deceased mother or grandmother or other relative, or a close friend, a war buddy, a child we loved, an angelic being, or even a loved animal. These, except for angels, have all passed through the Transition of death before us. They come to welcome us, the newly arrived, and guide us to our new home.

If we die when our body is old and it is our mother who comes to welcome us, we might expect Mother to look very aged—the mother of this old person! But instead she looks youthful and healthy, glowing and beautiful. When she died she would not care to continue to have an aging, ill, tired body. She left that behind to be burned or buried, and now in the Astral World, where thoughts and desires are the building tools, she has formed for herself with her own thoughts the type of body she really enjoys. For our sake, however, she may revert to some of the aspects of her earth-body that she knows will be familiar to us: certain clothing or the way her hair looks, for instance.

For the same reason—i.e., that the tools of the astral dimension are desire and thought—we, the newly dead, can let go of the old thoughts and feelings of illness, weakness, wounds, age, or handicaps—including mental retardation from any cause—and we can easily follow our own desires, the prayers of loved ones, or the instructions of a therapist to "stand up, firm and healthy, your shoulders back, your head up, your eyes bright, your mind clear—and *think* yourself strong and youthful!"

This method worked so well a number of times for me as the therapist that I took for granted it would always work as well. (Be wary of that word *always!*) When I was assisting the release of an obsessing entity, a man who had died alone, weak, and despairing at an advanced age, he simply *could not* imagine himself young and healthy. Having tried the quicker method outlined above with no results, I tempted him backward gradually through the years.

"Well, you say you are eighty-five. *Think* that you are only seventy-five. And now sixty-five . . . fifty-five . . . forty-five . . . thirty-five. . . ."

"Thirty-five!" he breathed ecstatically. And his despair was gone.

In cases in which the body was badly mutilated at death I follow the same general procedure. I tell the soul, "It was only your physical body that was crushed or wounded. That body is gone. You do not need it any more. Look at your body now, your astral body: see, it is whole and perfect. . . ." and so on.

One of the next events in our normal pathway after death is a *Review* of our entire life just ended as we see our thoughts, words, and activities in their entirety. This Review usually seems to be total: flashed into consciousness in every detail. Awareness of the reactions of others to our words, thoughts, and actions is also part of this Review, allowing us to perceive our influence on others throughout our lifetime. (You may recall the near-death experience of the criminal in Chapter Two. The Review after permanent death is a similar process for both beautiful deeds and ugly ones, as well as trivial ones.)

As the Review takes place we *judge* our own self, each thought, word, and deed, and evaluate its influence on other people. We come to definite conclusions: "I wasted my life, thinking of only myself, of nothing but money and power."

Or, "I did what I came to do; I feel satisfied." We note in what areas we were strong, in what others weak. We see in which aspects we were successful (in the spiritual sense) and in which others we still need development. These insights will be important in our planning for the next incarnation.

Either before or soon after the Review and the Judging, our soul experiences a *Cleansing*. This may be felt as an emotional catharsis or be experienced symbolically as purifying water, a holy fire, or a cleansing light. The metaphors and symbols vary but the effects are similar: the dispelling of dark feelings and shadows, the washing away of dross and heavy earth-holding negatives.

One of us, Vickie Mongrain, in her researches as she viewed psychically the progress of different souls, usually perceived the process as taking place in what she saw as a "Cleansing Room." Once when I was the subject in hypnosis, experiencing death as an East Indian peasant woman in a past life, I was drawn after my death toward a single shining yellow lotus blossom, hoping that its radiance would purify the contagion of a fatal disease from me. Vickie felt that the lotus symbolized the "Cleansing Room."

Not all of our unwanted negative traits and habits can be neutralized in this cleansing, of course, and it is possible that not all the souls that pass through the death-sequence need to undergo such a clearing.

In this book I have not usually tried to follow the souls much farther than this. A number of other therapists and researchers have done so—e.g., Joel Whitton, M.D., with Joe Fisher in their book *Life Between Life* (1983). Vickie and I began doing some sessions for research in that same year, with Vickie in hypnosis. She began eagerly questioning her deceased grandfather about conditions "on the other side." He became more and more reluctant about replying and finally told us explicitly that such things were not important. The important thing, he impressed upon us, was to live wisely and lovingly on *this* side, here and now. The Buddha likewise told his disciples, when they began to ask philosophical and theoretical questions, "Such questions lead not to edification"—are not important to one's spiritual education.

Nevertheless, being human and curious, we will always ask questions and seek answers. It is our human nature! And why not, so long as we *also* try earnestly to live well in the here and now? If we receive no definite answers, that is all right. If we get answers that we doubt and we try to discover whether or not they are accurate, that is all right. We cannot help wondering and wanting to know. The thing *most* important, however, is still how we live each day right now.

Environments After Death: The Astral World

Without thinking, we assume that after our body is dead our consciousness will still have much the same limitations and surroundings as in physical life. Any account of what we souls experience after leaving the body, people still in physical bodies expect to make good sense to their cognitive, reasoning minds and to feel familiar to them. When Robert Monroe attempts to explain to readers of his book, *Far Journeys* (1985), that souls on all levels communicate non-verbally by thoughts and impressions, he finds that he needs to make a kind of new language for his readers that *is* verbal.

Many earth-terms are inaccurate when one tries to apply them to non-physical realms: words like *higher, finer, plane, dimensions, region, place, day, years,* and other such terms. *Space, time,* and *direction* take on entirely new and different meanings in the non-physical worlds.

For example, can one ask how much a *thought* weighs, or whether the *idea* of a large object is bigger than the *idea* of a small object? Or whether a *thought* can go faster than light? Or whether an emotion, a desire, or a thought can pass through solid barriers? Attempts to combine two separate dimensions will produce a reduction to absurdity!

Yet, admitting all this, we need to have terms that are at least an attempt to describe to embodied people the adventures of our disembodied consciousness when we have left the physical body.

I shall use the widely accepted term "Astral Plane" for the next state after death, instead of the Rosicrucian term, "Desire World," or the Sanskrit word, "Kamaloka." Psychics in the modern world describe this plane simply as a higher vibratory rate superimposed upon and interpenetrating the slower vibrations of the physical matter of the earth-plane. It is easier for us to understand, however, if we follow the accepted symbolism of "lower" and "higher" planes (or levels or dimensions) when speaking of the astral, mental, and still higher invisible worlds. Clairvoyants speak of the Astral Plane as being divided into three major "levels" with smaller divisions within each of the major ones. Data from hypnotic post-death experiences agree.

Some clairvoyant descriptions of the Astral ("starry") Plane are very beautiful, emphasizing the fluidity and malleability of the astral substance into lovely forms and scenery by the thoughts and desires of the souls inhabiting the plane:

"The matter is almost living. It is in unceasing motion, fluid, taking all imaginable and unimaginable forms with inconceivable rapidity and facility, at the same time coruscating and scintillating in a thousand ever-changing shades of color, incomparable to anything we know in this physical state of consciousness. . . ."

Clairvoyant friends tell us that this type of description applies only to the Middle and Upper Astral levels and is too idyllic for the lower regions of the astral world. In the Lower Astral the sordid thoughts and other negatives of its inhabitants dim the colors, darken the brightness, and cloud the purity of the luminous tints so that these lower realms are dark and unpleasant.

The Astral Levels

You may recall a simple experiment in high school Physics, in which a mixture of *oil, sand,* and *iron-filings* was shaken up in *water* in a test-tube and set aside for a moment. The heavy iron-filings immediately sank to the bottom; the light oil droplets floated to the top; and the sand settled down on top of the iron-filings, leaving the water above that, so that there were four layers in the test-tube instead of the one dirty-looking mixture.

In quite a similar way do human souls separate into different astral "layers" after death. Souls heavy with long-time habits of hate, anger, cruelty, or greed find themselves going to the lower astral levels; the saintly and the kindly wise ones find themselves in the top levels; and the rest of us find our appropriate levels in between. Or, to express it another way, it is at this point that the after-death pathway divides into several different branches, each branch a "normal" pathway for the types of souls that find themselves drawn to follow it.

No strict Judge nor punitive Deity orders us which path to take, which level to go to. Our own character is the deciding factor; not just a single deed, whether good or bad, but the deep-rooted traits and habits of the whole life are what count.

The Lower Astral Levels

To follow the tarnished souls first: As each soul has already reviewed and judged its own life, action by action, and has come to this, its "appropriate" level, in this level each creates its own individual private type of hell: according to the despair and suffering its callousness caused others, so will be its own misery in the private hell it has created. *Each soul does receive what it has given to others.* This is not merely a religious teaching. It is the law of Nature in the Spiritual World. (A good example is the description of the near-death life-review of the criminal whose case is reported by Dr. Lorimer in Chapter Two.) But for even the worst characters there is always opportunity to change the nature and to rise to a higher vibration, a higher astral level. No lake of fire nor hell of eternal torment has been found.

I wish to quote briefly from *Life Between Life* by Whitton and Fisher (pp. 98 and 106), about a soul in the (astral) interlife:

(Michael's) self-reproach was beyond the reach of reassurance.

"What do you see?" Dr. Whitton asked once more. Slowly, painfully, Michael replied. . . .

"It is black and I will not look. There was much I could have done but did not. I could have done so much good, but . . . I did not."

To experience remorse in the life between lives is to experience a form of hell. For there is a time—quite early on, according to most subjects—when guilt comes home to roost in all its raw ugliness, stripped of the rationalizations and excuses we all employ to explain away our failings. This hell, however, is not eternal damnation. When the past life is assessed, the compassionate encouragement of the judgment board allows us to perceive even our most reprehensible actions with a degree of sympathy.

No matter how misused the immediate past life has been, the oversoul knows there's always another chance to make amends.

"I have been allowed," (Michael) said, speaking of his visits to the interlife, "the barest glimpse of levels of creation that are far above anything that I can even begin to put into words. I was made to feel that everything that we do has meaning at the highest level. Our sufferings are not random; they are merely part of an eternal plan more complex and awe-inspiring than we are capable of imagining."

Some souls after death find themselves not in a "hell" but in a colorless dark or gray expanse, usually chilly, often alone or feeling alone even if the presence of others is sensed. This is either before or just after the Review. It is to a condition like this that souls gravitate if they are still weighed down (at least temporarily) by emotions like grief, bewilderment, fear, doubt, feelings of unworthiness or guilt. These emotions act like "sinkers" attached to the soul. There is no keen suffering—only the seemingly endless grayness. Other souls that gravitate here may have committed suicide or may have had no previous thinking about an afterlife, or no belief in the persistence of consciousness after death, or else a lifelong habit of looking at the dark side of everything. Others may be those incapable of feeling tenderness or gratitude. This type of condition is one, but not the lowest, of the Lower Astral Levels.

The Middle Astral Levels

Most souls find themselves in a beautiful, peaceful setting, as Cox, the gunner, did, and as "wee Mary" did, waking out of her death-sleep to look up and see her deceased father and being carried out into the flowers and sunshine. These are examples of what is called the *Middle Astral* realm, to which most well-meaning decent people gravitate naturally. They feel quite at home, literally. Their earth-habituated thoughts and enjoyments build for them pleasant earthlike scenes peopled with flowers, animals, birds like those that they enjoyed on earth. The pets that they loved join them there after the pets die.

An example of a soul who suddenly discovered his new astral environment was the consciousness of a young man

nick-named "Rutabaga," a ranchhand in the early years of
the Ken Caryl ranch near Denver. He had been killed while
trying to train a wild horse and his mind had remained in the
vicinity ("I live here," he said), unaware of the changes the
passing years had brought to the ranch. When—through the
young woman who had felt his ghostly presence—I described the freedom of the next stage for him in contrast to
the limitations of his earth-bound state, the channel and I
almost felt his "Wow!" of sudden understanding. Without
bothering to thank us or to say good-bye, he broke contact
with us and rushed off like a kid let out of school. We *felt* his
delight trailing behind him—his ideas of fulfilling all his
wishes by manipulating the astral "substance" by his
thoughts and desires!

I think I should have called him back to explain to him
that the astral world is not merely a playground but a learning environment for a period of assimilating the spiritual
lessons of the life just past. This was before I had learned that
my calling him urgently would have brought him back.
Anyway, he escaped. That Rutabaga is one happy irrespon-
sible young cowboy out there somewhere!

The Upper Astral Levels

The Upper Astral Levels are still more beautiful, both
visually and psychologically. Here, I believe, is the prototype
for that idyllic "place" that has been called the Happy Hunting Ground, the Elysian Fields, Paradise, the Summerland. It
is still in the Desire World. Souls gravitating here find existence so delightful that they may choose to remain a long time
(as we know time). There is so much beauty, so much freedom and joy! Edith Cox's description of her after-death state
as being "full of light and laughter" and her feelings of
jubilant freedom indicate an Upper Astral state for her—not
at all surprising to anyone who knew her in earth-life.

The Upper Astral regions are still regions in which there is the working out of earthly desires, wants, and needs. Even unselfish and spiritual desires, if subtly encased in self-seeking attitudes such as hope for a personal reward or for thanks and appreciation, will hold a soul here in the Astral Plane for a while, until these desires have either been outgrown and put by or else have been fulfilled and laid to rest.

The Mental Planes

After completing the appropriate learning time in the Astral World, the soul is ready to graduate to the Mental World, and it experiences what has been called the *Second Death*—more like a promotion—laying aside the astral body and rising, as the mind, the consciousness, into the next dimension.

The Mental Plane's lower level is called the Concrete Mental Plane; the upper one (also called the *Causal Plane)* is the Abstract Mental Plane. It is on the causal level that all the experiences of the earth-life and the learning of the Astral Planes are processed and condensed into traits, talents, and tendencies and become a "kernel" or "seed" for the entity to take back into the next earth-life as its individual *Predispositions.*

It is on the Causal Level that the entity "rests in the Lord" for a timeless time, until it is "time" for it to reincarnate. Here it is not the personality but the Higher Self, the Soul, which is the entity.

We are told repeatedly that the "higher" levels are invisible only because the vibrations and the frequencies are higher than those of earth molecules—that *there is no spatial distance.* Our dead are still "here," only living at a higher vibratory rate. There is not a departing or a passing away in the sense of spatial traveling. There is instead a definite shift in the ability to sense and perceive, as if the psyche of the one freed from the body has become deaf to the earth-range of sounds and is now aware of octaves above; is no longer able to see earth-colors and objects and bodies but is aware of indescribable "colors" of infrared and ultraviolet—all these changes occurring in the same "space" as occupied by persons in physical bodies.

"Assumptions" Here Do Not Precede, They Follow

One may ask, "How do you know all this about Planes and Levels is true? Maybe people have just made up these schemes."

Yes, and even if the ideas are dignified (and doubted) by the term "Philosophical Assumptions," the question is still valid. But let us ask, also, how the ideas first came to be, long ago, and why similar ideas have been springing up in various places and being "discovered" by different workers in different places today. Not only the ancient Tibetans and ancient Egyptians who wrote *Books of the Dead* but modern workers like Lord Hugh Dowding and his group in London after World War II, and George Meek (*After We Die, What Then?*), and various others all find similar sequences for souls after death of the physical body.

In my own years of work with hypnosis I have accumulated many thick notebooks of handwritten notes taken down as nearly verbatim as possible during sessions of one to three hours, many dealing with experiences of the client's present life situations, some with prenatal experiences, some with past-life experiences or relationships, and some with death-experiences. It is from these last that I selected a few to include in this book. Of all the death-experiences, some were continued into the after-death stages, and these fell into categories, such as various pleasant conditions, some unpleasant conditions, rather gray neutral ones, and so on.

Then one would be tempted to give each class a name, for convenience. Or else, one might decide to label the classes with names that other persons in the past had used for what seem like similar past-death conditions.

The sequence, you see, is first the discovery and observation of such differing categories. Second is the naming of each. And only third is a theory proposed and a "Philosophical Assumption" propounded—which to the researcher sounds rather ludicrous, when the *primary observations* are the basis for this nebulous armchair type of "philosophizing" an "assumption."

This book, then, records what we—a good many of us now—have been finding in our modern work with patients and clients and discovering how neatly our findings fit into those described by workers of long ago. So we adopt the names given by some of those ancient workers to the states we now are re-discovering for our souls' journeys after death.

Summary

Normally, then, the stages of the soul's journey after death are about as follows:

1. The body feels weaker, more tired and heavy. The mind may remain clear, but the body refuses to respond or move. It may appear comatose.
2. The mind sees the body, observes it, usually from a position above. The mind can move freely. It feels, "I am *here*, not in that body there."
3. The mind (soul) sees and hears the persons near but is unable to communicate with them.
4. The consciousness (soul) withdraws from the earth-scene and perceives a Light which welcomes it. De-

ceased friends or relatives are also seen coming to welcome and escort the soul.

5. There is a *Review* of the life just past, including the ways in which the soul influenced others for good or ill.

6. The soul *judges* its own actions and thoughts; it sees its strengths and weaknesses.

7. The soul gravitates to an *appropriate Astral Level* where it will assimilate what it has learned during the past earth-life and learn new lessons for a future life.

8. The soul eventually passes through the *Second Death,* graduating into the *Mental Plane* first to the Concrete Mental, then into the Abstract Mental (Causal) Level, where, as the immortal Soul, it rests and "ripens" until it chooses to begin another descent into a new incarnation.

9. The newborn brings with it certain *Predispositions*— i.e., the condensed talents and tendencies derived from the past lives—and also the portions of karma, both negative and positive, that it has chosen to work on in this coming earth-life, meeting souls it has known in past lives.

10. Each earth-life offers many opportunities to increase the strength, love, courage, and wisdom of the soul and also opportunities to make restitution to others injured in the past. It also gives free will in all matters of choice.

Now just for fun, why don't we re-read this list in first person and see how it feels? I think we'll feel that it is a pretty good fit!

6

ABNORMAL SEQUENCES
AFTER DEATH

MANY ARE THE WAYS in which the physical body can die.
Fewer are the emotional patterns of dying. If the final feelings are relief, gladness, resignation, or peacefulness, the
soul moves easily out of the body and sees the Light and
moves into it at once or is pulled into it, thus following the
normal sequence into the Astral World.

If, however, the final emotions of the dying are fear or
guilt, hate or rage, despair or futility, or a sense of incom-
pleteness, these emotions produce a mind-set away from the
naturalness of dying and tend toward an abnormal sequence
of post-death events. Many—multitudes—of souls, especially in these violent materialistic centuries, do not find
themselves following the normal pathway. Not being mentally or spiritually prepared for death before it occurs, they
are bewildered, perplexed, emotionally confused after they
see their dead body from an outside point of view and yet
feel *themselves* conscious and alive.

For a time the consciousness of the deceased may stay
close to the body, or may think of going to its former home or
to a familiar place like a park or bar. The very *thought* or *desire*,
the *wish*, draws the soul to that place, and the change is so
easy and natural that the soul may hardly realize that it did

99

not travel in the familiar earthly manner. In the new location the disembodied mind finds the same frustrating condition of affairs as in the death-bed room: hears and sees the people there and attempts to contact them, to communicate with them, and finds itself totally ignored. Especially when the deceased soul is that of a child the situation is pathetic.

Wanderers

Most such souls eventually begin to wander in a colorless intermediate state and are called "earth-bound," close enough to the physical dimension for them to see and hear the living while the living are unable to see or hear them. Frustrated and lonely, ignored by relatives and friends, they may see a Light but do not know what it indicates. Some simply ignore it or feel mildly curious, but start to wander away, aimlessly or toward some particular place or person.

Some, seeing the Light, do tend to gravitate toward it but then turn back to the earth-plane, either because they feel strongly that they still have a certain task to complete or are drawn back by the prayers and grief of loved ones—or, conversely, want to remain with their loved ones, hoping to help and comfort them.

All of these remain earth-bound, their consciousness staying close to the former thought-patterns and feeling-habits of physical life. This is an abnormal situation for the simple reason that the disembodied psyche cannot communicate freely with persons in physical embodiment. Even the souls that remain close to earth for good reasons, such as to finish an incomplete task or to comfort loved ones, are unable to accomplish these goals because of the almost complete lack of communication.

Fear is perhaps one of the most common negative emotions that keep a soul earth-bound, and the fear of going to hell is one of the main reasons for this terror. Hell-fire sermons do much harm. It is *not a rare condition* for a soul to become a Wanderer because, convinced by sermons or by life-style that he or she is not good enough for heaven and knowing no other alternative than hell, the soul stays in this intermediate state, earth-bound. One man, contacted after death, is said to have commented, "Well, if this is heaven, I'm surprised, and if it is hell, it is better than I expected."

During my (channeled) conversation with an old gunslinger who had been shot and killed, he recoiled when his attention was directed toward the Light. He began to shout, "Oh, no, you're not going to get me to go into that light! No, sir! You can't get me into that light!"

He would not listen to my attempted explanations, continuing to shout, "That light would burn me up. You can't *make* me go into it!"

I interrupted loudly, "I tell you, it is not a destroying fire, it is entirely different! Why do you seem to think it is like the fire of hell?"

"Well, I've been bad. . . ."

"Why do you say you've been bad?"

"Well, I lied—and cheated —and stole—and killed . . . and—uh—I was bad with women." (The channel said afterward that he cleaned up his language a little for my sake!)

The scene of his death had been typical of some Old West movies: a bar, men half-drunk, a youth swaggering in boasting of his prowess and threatening the old gun-slinger. When the boy pointed his gun at the old man, the latter drew swiftly, the two fired at almost the same moment, and both were killed.

"He got me," admitted the old man, "but I proved I was still quick on the draw. I got him before I fell."

I urged him to sweep out of himself all the fears, the boastfulness, the lying and stealing and killing habits, "and get rid of the alcoholism, too. Just clean yourself up. Get rid of everything you don't want to carry with you into the next life. Are you doing this?"

He nodded—somewhat to my surprise. It is easier to convince entities after their death than it is to persuade them before death!

"And Pete, you got Mike, and he got you. Why don't you call Mike and make friends with him? It's all over now."

At that moment a high boyish voice came from the channel, "Hey, Pete, you old reprobate! Whatcha doin' down there? Come on up and have some fun!" (Our *thoughts* about Mike had called him to us, as is normal in the Astral World.)

I asked Mike to come and shake hands with Pete. He did so, and the two went off together toward the Light. As they went I called after them, "Pete, why don't you get rid of that attitude of being 'bad with women,' too?"

"Yeah, I think that'd be a good idea," came the sheepish reply. "You're a character, Louise."

"So are you, Pete," I retorted, suppressing a chuckle. "So long."

Entirely different was the abnormal state of some of the twelve hundred or more Muslim pilgrims who had been killed when a tunnel collapsed as they were leaving Mecca after having visited their holy shrine. We asked first for a spokesman for the group that had not yet found their way to the next plane. (The channel said that many had already gone.)

To the spokesman I explained what had happened and what now needed to be done: that they, the souls of the dead, needed to look for the Light and move toward and into it. As soon as I mentioned the word "death" they began to understand and were ready to move on fearlessly. The spokesman said, "We accept your help so graciously given. Allah be praised! We go now."

Then a different voice asked, through the channel, "What if some do not wish to go?"

I asked the name of the one who had spoken. It was a woman who wanted to find her husband and her son before going on. I asked her to check among the souls there, to find if her husband and son were among them.

"I do not see them," she said, after a moment.

"Then let your soul look among the living. Are they still alive?"

There was a pause. Then, philosophically, "I guess we do not have to wait, do we."

I assured her that it was all right for her to go on with the others. I seemed to sense that to her menfolk she, a woman, was chiefly a servant and care-giver, hardly a soul in her own right, and she felt free now to go without them.

As these left, I inquired if there were any others remaining.

Another voice, a man's, replied, "What if we were not supposed to die? What if this was a mistake, and I was supposed to live and finish my work?" He declared that he had been born and called to do a certain work on earth and had not completed it. He insisted that his death was premature, a true accident, and now that his body, his vehicle, was dead, he felt that his consciousness needed to remain and finish the task through someone else.

Not knowing how to argue with him, I asked for a spiritual counselor of his own faith to come and give the man's soul advice. There was a considerable pause. When no one answered, I asked my own spiritual advisor if he would offer some suggestions. After a brief pause, Master Ching's voice, quiet and firm, spoke: "Tell him, 'There is nothing lost. There is no delay. He will go on, and will come back and finish the work the better for having had this experience.'"

The channel, feeling the emotions of the man, said that he was comforted by the reassurance but was shocked by the words, "He will come back." The idea of returning to the earth was foreign to him.

These cases illustrate several of the reasons for souls' remaining near the earth plane.

Poltergeists

Other Wanderers, trying to establish communication with the living, attempt to attract attention by moving physical objects, making noises, interfering with electrical connections, and causing other peculiar and inexplicable phenomena. These are called *Poltergeists*, "playful spirits." Very few are dangerous. Most are simply amusing themselves or trying to get people's attention or the help they need. Sometimes their frustration does cause them to become malicious. It is said that many perform their distracting antics in houses where an adolescent girl lives, but this is by no means true in all cases.

A few years ago all the electrical appliances in my house seemed to be giving trouble at the same time. The vacuum cleaner would turn itself off after I turned it on. Electric clocks and radios stopped working properly. Even the ignition of my car gave trouble.

I asked a psychic friend if there was a poltergeist in my house. Carroll meditated a moment. "Yes, I see a small figure in the door of your kitchen. It is not dangerous, just wants to play. I think it is a child."

Then through automatic writing she received, "This is a small boy who died in a fire. His name is Conrad. He does not know he is dead. He enjoys watching Dr. Louise and likes her house. Call him, explain how he died, and when you hear him say, 'I understand,' call his mother. Her name is Elvira; she is on this side. She will take care of him from there."

I went home, wondering how I would know when Conrad understood, for I do not "hear"; I am not clair-audient. I chose a position in which I could sit and not be observed by any passing neighbor who might wonder why I was talking to the empty air. I did call Conrad and tell him about the fire and how he lost his body and now was free.

When I felt that even a very stupid child would surely have understood, I called Elvira and asked her to take charge of her son. I waited. I could not tell that anything had changed.

Nothing went wrong with electrical appliances after that anyway—but I did wish that I had asked Conrad to fix, before he left, all the things he had unfixed. It cost me about two hundred dollars to have everything repaired!

One other time I suspected that a poltergeist was in my home. This was a few years after the encounter with Conrad, so I felt more confident about the situation. I asked a co-worker to channel the entity to find out whether the electrical problems in my household were again due to "other-side" interference.

A child, another small boy, was contacted. During the conversation I explained that we could not see or hear him; I asked him to think back to the last time that people like us, in living bodies, could see and hear him. He began to scream. He screamed and screamed! (The channel told me afterward that she could hear the screaming coming from her mouth but she had no control over it.)

I knew instantly what was wrong: I had neglected to say those extremely important words, *"without pain or fear"* when I asked him to go back to that former time.

Hastily I ordered, *"Let your mind come out of your body and be safe here with us. Just look down and see, as an observer without pain or fear,* what is happening to that boy's body down there."

He quieted, though still sobbing softly, as he told of playing with other boys on an empty railroad flat-car which was one of a chain on a siding. An engine farther up the track backed into the chain to attach it and the sudden slight jar caused the lad to fall off the flat-bed with his legs across the track. The legs were run over slowly as the car moved, one leg being completely amputated. Adults heard the children's screams, came, carried the boy and his leg back to his home, where his mother, seeing her son this way, began to cry.

More tears burst out now. "I don't want her to cry," he wept.

Again I asked him to see events from a safe withdrawn position as an observer, and now to let his mind "expand" to find the doctor and see if the doctor was coming. The answer was, "No, the doctor was driving his buggy into the country to attend the birth of a baby; he could not be reached."

Quietly now the lad slipped into death from loss of blood.

"Now go to the moment when your soul leaves your body and tell me about that," I said, using the usual formula for a death experience.

He said the usual things: cessation of pain, seeing his body below and his mother weeping over it, feeling much calmer, though vainly trying to comfort his mother, and finally wandering off. About nine years old, he quickly adjusted to his new condition and began to roam freely, looking for amusement. He came to my house and found it interesting.

I reminded him reproachfully that he had caused me much trouble and some expense, naming some of the problems with various appliances.

He began to cry again. "I didn't mean any harm. I didn't mean to make trouble. I only wanted to do what *you* did; I just *pushed* things."

Bless his little urchin heart. I comforted him, explained his present situation and asked him to look for a Light (yes, he could see it: "It's all around.") and to watch for someone who might come to meet him.

"It's my mother!" The tears now were happy tears. It was a joyous reunion. (His mother had died in the meantime.)

Ghosts

Like poltergeists, *ghosts* can be put into the general category of Wanderers, whether they remain in one location or are more or less on the loose. Some souls remain close to the scene of the body's demise or the vicinity of its burial for a considerable period. Clairvoyants and persons with etheric vision tell us that they see disembodied entities in funeral parlors, in cemeteries, and at the locations of fatal accidents. Some of these may be mindless wraiths, the decaying "etheric" part of the bodies. Others of the entities tend to relive the traumatic crisis over and over, endlessly. It is probable that many of these are only *partial consciousnesses* of the deceased, as the teachings of the Hawaiian Huna might say: probably the "low mind," the subconsciousness, lacking insight and logical reasoning.

Mentally and astrally, ghosts are lost. There is rarely anything to be feared from ghosts; most of them need as much help as we can give them. Through a channel we can contact them and learn who they are, how they died, and assist them to move on into the appropriate astral level, "to your own true home."

I suppose that the cowboy, "Rutabaga," could be considered a ghost, though he was not *seen*. He was *felt* as a strong presence and a chilly sensation. The cold feeling associated with ghosts and reported by numerous persons is, I believe, the result of the entity's drawing energy (of warmth) from any living body that happens to be nearby. Nan Taylor told her ESP students that only dark entities caused a cold feeling, but when she herself visited our meditation group (invisibly, in her astral body), we all felt a chilly sensation, and two or three of us were certain that it was Nan's presence. I had no conviction of the identity of the presence either way, but I did feel the coldness. Nan later confirmed by telephone that she had checked on us. I think it is a matter of the drawing out of heat-energy rather than any "radiation of cold" from a dark being.

I have dealt matter-of-factly with a few so-called ghosts that were reported to me by clients or friends. In one case, the complaint was of a coldness that constantly pervaded one certain corner of an upstairs room of the house in which the client was living with her family. When she went into hypnosis and I called "the entity who is in the corner of the upstairs room" of the house at the address given, a tired old man replied. He had been a wino with no job, and he simply half-starved and eventually died in that room. Not knowing what else to do, he just stayed there. We helped him to divest himself of that "dirty old overcoat of sadness and loneliness with the pockets heavy with alcoholism and negative feelings of futility and anger," and to move on in the company of the loved one who came to meet him.

One of my coworkers became so enthusiastic about all the Colorado ghost stories recorded in a book she had, that she wanted us to begin contacting and helping as many ghosts as we could! I was too occupied to start at that time, and when I did have time, she was the one who was too busy. So our project was never realized. Perhaps some of my readers will be able to contact and assist the Colorado ghosts some day.

The first ghost I dealt with (although I did not think of it as a ghost then) was in 1980 or '81 in the house next to my country home. My neighbor said that she could not get rid of a stain at the bottom of the staircase. She could scrub it away but it would come back. She told me that a woman had been murdered in that house years before she moved in. At that time I did not know how to go about helping the ghostly presence. All I could do was to meditate for the entity, assure it of its value in the universe (as every being is), and to ask it to vacate the house and move on. This amateurish attempt seemed to help somewhat; I did not follow up to find out details.

Indian burial grounds that have been desecrated by being over-built by modern buildings are not infrequently said to be haunted. One such is a restaurant outside of Cedaredge, my former hometown. It has had about six different owners in the years since it was built, and people who have worked there such as cooks or waitresses tell of strange happenings, odd noises, nuisance activity, such as flour being thrown around on the kitchen floor at night, and so on. Why did I not "clear" the place? Well, one is reluctant to go up to a strange person, the manager, and offer to eject a ghost. Now if the manager had *asked*, that would be different.

One of the first *roving Wanderers* that we encountered and "rescued" came into my house during a small group meeting of friends. After we came out of meditation two of the ladies spoke of having been aware of a man who had entered through the (closed) front door. One of the women said she merely observed and decided he was not intending to harm or trouble us and she then ignored his presence, but the other woman said he had no right to barge in like that and she mentally ordered him to leave. He did.

I was rather surprised and not too pleased at her reaction. It was my house and I did not want to expel someone without knowing who he was and why he had come. I suggested that we ask him to return and tell us about himself through a channel. One of the other ladies volunteered to be the channel.

The man returned and in a few short sentences told his story. He had been a loner with no family and no friends except for his horse. The horse, after successfully crossing a long railroad bridge (quite a feat for a horse), stumbled on a loose rock and the man was thrown off, his head striking a stone.

Between sobs he said, "Brownie wouldn't leave. She stayed there by my body for two weeks and nearly starved before someone found us. They shot Brownie and took away my body. . . ."

When I asked if he had seen Brownie on the other side, he said no—but then he exclaimed, "There she is! She's coming!" (Our *thoughts* of her had called her to us.)

He could not speak any more, ducking his head to hide tears—that is, the channel's head was lowered and tears were trickling down her cheeks. I asked what was happening.

"Brownie has her head down—on my shoulder—My arm is around her neck. . . ." He was reunited with his only friend.

I reminded him of the keen intelligence of horses. "Brownie knows the way to go. She will take you home." I felt confident that the love and trust between man and horse—strong positive feelings directing toward the Light—were sufficient compass and escort into the next realm.

(In a later session with a different client I did not trust the horse to be the guide for the deceased owner, because the man had considered the animal only a means of transportation, not a friend.)

Obsessing Entities

Among the earth-bound Wanderers many sooner or later find and move into an area that seems lighter or warmer than the gray chilliness in which they have been roving—an area which turns out to be the warmth of a living physical body, especially if the body is sick, hurt, weak, shocked, old, or stressed, and the protecting aura is "open."

There are several degrees of closeness that can be distinguished between the attached entity and the host, although some therapists use the term "possession" to include all of the following:

1. For a relatively loose relationship when the entity is outside the host's body but is near the aura, the term is "shadowing" or "influencing."
2. "Oppression" is the term when the entity, as seen clairvoyantly, is inside the aura of the host or is affecting the host intermittently or mildly. Another term for either of these is "harassing" (Naegeli-Osjord).
3. "Obsession" is the condition of the invasion of the physical body of the host by the entity, who brings with it all its own personality traits, including any that are undesirable, often perplexing the host.
4. "Possession" is the complete take-over of the host's body and the expulsion of the host's own mind, the invading entity now using the body to exhibit its own behaviors and speak its own words. There may be alternation between complete possession and partial possession (obsession). Many cases of full possession are probably confined in mental institutions or prisons because the changes in personality and behavior are dramatic and conspicuous. Full possession is rare. (I have witnessed only one case, and that occurred without warning in my own therapy room when my young co-worker's body was taken over briefly.)

Obsession, on the other hand, is far more common and less frequently suspected. Neither the host nor the invading entity may be aware of the parasitic relationship. In some cases, however, the invading entity has entered purposely, "to protect her" or "to feel safe," for instance, although it is seldom aware that it brings its own personality into the host—its own habits, thought patterns, addictions, and so on—confusing the victim, even causing him to wonder if he is going crazy. Physical and psychological problems due to an obsessing entity are not amenable to medical treatment. Such entities are not Multiple Personalities of the living person and cannot be successfully integrated with the client's own personality.

Such an obsessing entity can be questioned through the host-person's own mind and vocal apparatus and the story of its life and death obtained. The host person is the channel in these cases. A third person in meditation or hypnosis at any distance may also become a channel for the obsessed victim if need be. (Irene Hickman, D.O., prefers this method of "Remote Depossession.") The stories related by obsessing entities that I have released from my clients are first-person experiences, each one different, each told with simplicity and directness, often with emotion and pain if these were present in the death experience and if the therapist does not control them verbally with instructions to be free of pain. Remember my little poltergeist boy?)

These Wanderers who become obsessing entities are not Guides or Masters, for high souls do not invade, unless in very exceptional circumstances for a brief time and for reasons dedicated to benefiting the host. Most obsessing entities are not evil either; they are lonely unhappy souls who "did not know where to go" when they found themselves still conscious after death. They are the "lost souls," the "poor souls," we hear about in our religions—not condemned, just lost.

The opportunity for a Wanderer to move into a living person's body or aura is usually during an "open" moment when the victim is under the influence of anesthesia during an operation or has been using drugs or alcohol; when his system has been jarred off balance by an accident or a strong emotion; or merely from a similarity of personality or circumstances; sometimes just because the host person was "there" nearby.

There are literally dozens of reasons given by obsessing entities for entering a living person. No type of living person is exempt. People who work with the public tend to be vulnerable—nurses, doctors, counselors, healers—but no one is exempt, although most are totally unaware of any such invasion.

I myself turned out to have been unknowingly entertaining an entity, as I discovered when I attended a workshop by Dr. William Baldwin in 1985. No one else in the group had offered to be a volunteer, so I raised my hand even though I felt sure I had no "entity" in *me!* The demonstration was an eye-opener for me more than for anyone else, I do not doubt. I had selected this workshop to gain more knowledge of what to do for the patients who had come to me for odd symptoms that did suggest obsession. I learned much in the workshop that I needed to know, and I filled in later with books such as Dr. Carl Wickland's *Thirty Years Among the Dead.*

The entity that Bill Baldwin contacted in me was a young horse-groom in the stable of one of England's queens. He incurred the queen's displeasure for objecting to going along with a project of hers: "My Lady, you have honor, you have majesty. You are above this." Her response after a day or so was to order his execution. (It was the dead weight of his bodily and emotional feelings that had added to my own during the long years when I was struggling with "Chronic Fatigue Syndrome.") Gently Baldwin persuaded the young groom that, far from being unworthy to go to a bright place in the spiritual world, he had proved his worthiness by remaining true to his own highest ideals. The groom had felt that if his adored queen considered him unworthy to live, he certainly was not worthy to go to any heavenly place in death. So he had remained earth-bound, being attracted to "Louise" as a kindred spirit, but not entering her until at the age of twenty-six she suffered, like him, a profound disillusionment in a dear friend (similarity of circumstances).

The entities becoming attached to living persons include both sexes and every age, from every country and from any historical period. They may enter any living person, male or female, child, adult, or aged. Until we contact them and ask about their lives and deaths, we have no way of guessing who or what type they may be or why they are parasitizing. Many turn out to be relatives, either in the present life or in a past life.

When a psychic friend suggested that just for fun we see if any obsessing entity was in her, I contacted a female who admitted that she was old. Asked her name, she reeled off her full triple name quite proudly. Asked why she went into Carroll, she responded in a tone that implied that I ought to know already and that she had a perfect right to enter: "She's my *granddaughter!*"

Asked why she chose Carroll out of all her relatives, she said huffily, "She's the only one who didn't care about my money!"

She said that after passing away quietly in the hospital she followed her granddaughter and when Carroll was seated in the airplane for her return home after the funeral, the grandmother "just sat down on her lap, and went in." In spite of being very psychic about other people's affairs, Carroll had no inkling of all this.

After returning to full consciousness, Carroll said, "Let me tell you about Grandmother's money. She had plenty, and she loved to control people by her money. If someone didn't do as she wanted, she would threaten to cut them out of her will. One day she said something like that to me, and I said, 'Grandma, I don't want your old money. If you gave me even one dollar, I'd throw it on the floor and stamp on it!' I guess that impressed her."

Yes, it really had impressed Grandma; it won her respect. She said that another reason she had chosen Carroll was because "she laughs and has fun; I wanted some of that."

So sometimes an obsession begins because the living person has qualities that are desired by the incoming invader. As another entity said about the man he had entered, "He's a go-getter. I figured he'd do the work and I'd just ride along."

In some cases the soul does not wander but goes at once after death to a chosen place or person, just as Carroll's grandmother did, and just as another entity did into me. This latter case was doubly interesting to me because I was informed by a grandmother-entity whom I was releasing from a young woman, "Louise, you still have one in you—a woman, dark—not black—Japanese. Her name is Akiu Hitana. Akiu Hitana." (On the astral level, and even in the earth-bound level, the souls can see what we cannot.) Three times she pronounced the name clearly, and I wrote it as nearly phonetically as I could.

A few weeks later I was able to have a coworker contact Akiu Hitana, calling her by name while I lay in hypnosis. I learned that she was the tiny stooped Japanese lady with whom I had spent an hour or two in her country home in Idaho while my car was being repaired. Unable to talk in a common language, still we conversed by signs and smiles. When my car was brought back I said good-bye to her, leaving as a gift a book of photographs of Hawaii (as the nearest thing to Japan that I had) and a small magnifying glass, which I showed her how to use on the pictures. That was the one and only time I had been with her. I felt that she was very lonely here in this foreign land, where even her son refused to speak in Japanese with her. When she died she must have felt that I was the person closest to her, and she sought me out and somehow moved in.

"She doesn't think of me very often," I heard the sad little voice coming from my mouth. It was true; I very seldom had. (Her thoughts were received as *thoughts*. If she thought in Japanese, I heard them as English.)

She said her name meant "Sunshine on the Grass." And she hoped to go home to Japan now that she knew she should not be in me. When my coworker directed her toward the Light she asked wistfully, "Will it be like Japan?"

Assured that it would be just like Japan but more beautiful, she started to go and then cried joyfully, "My husband! And my baby!"

"And you can be with them now. Run, if you like," suggested my coworker.

"Oh, no, that would not be dignified," said the little lady. (I have thought of her repeatedly since this session. I believe she must be thinking of me, too.)

The death experiences of these attached souls are not different from those of Wanderers or those of clients' past-life deaths, and they have the same wide spread of ways in which they occurred. One notes, however, that the mind-set of the person dying is not directed toward the Light; the emotions and thoughts are on the negative or at least the earthly side, sad or lonely, not calm, peacefully accepting, or happy.

How do we avoid being invaded and parasitized without our knowledge? Chiefly by keeping our aura clear of the negative feelings and emotions as far as is possible, keeping our thoughts positive so that our mental body is also clear, and spending a little time daily in meditation. Visualizing light around and within us is helpful, but only if our daily thoughts, words, and feelings are gradually brought into light as well. It is wise to keep up a mild, quiet long-lasting pressure rather than to try a crash-course into spirituality! Even that is a help, however.

There are some special cases in which a soul has gone to the Light but has been pulled back and becomes earth-bound or even becomes an obsessing soul.

Such was the situation with a minister. Before his death he had always done all the business work and figuring of taxes, expenses, and so on. After his death his wife tried to do all these things, and would often say, "Oh, Honey, I need you to tell me what to do about this. I wish you were here to help me." Her repeated yearnings and her loneliness drew him back irresistibly. He tried to help her but could not reach her mentally; instead he found himself drawn inside her as an obsessing entity.

When I spoke to him (his wife in hypnosis and channeling) he said that he had been to the Light but was back in the earth plane.

"Oh, it has been so hard," he murmured in a weak voice.

Not only the husband was in the wife but also her mother, a sister, an aunt, and a dear woman friend were in her. At the end of the session, I commented, "It sounded like a family reunion!"

She laughed, and then clutched at her chest. For a moment I thought she was having cardiac pains until she said, "Oh, I feel so light! I didn't know I was carrying such a burden."

7

NORMALIZING
THE ABNORMAL

THESE ENTITIES, lost, lonely, wandering, or else cooped up in some living person's body, need assistance to get to a better state of being, and we, the living, are the connecting link. One of our group, Cynthia, asked Mother Mary during meditation why, with all the power at Mary's command, she did not simply do the work of rescuing herself and not wait until we in mortal bodies went to work. The answer was that Mary's vibratory rate (power) is so extremely high that it could only with difficulty be lowered to the requisite level without a middle step, a transformer, so to speak. And we in living bodies are that transformer, whether we pray, meditate, talk to the souls, or use hypnosis.

This is an answer somewhat similar to one that Dr. Bill Baldwin received from a high being to a similar question during the Releasement of a negative entity. The high being said that a negative *energy* in the client was perceived, but it could not be recognized by the high being as an invasive *entity* needing to be released until the contact was established with the client in hypnosis so that Baldwin could converse with both the high being and the dark entity. Baldwin was the intermediary.

Therefore, in addition to asking in prayer for the Rescue or the Releasement that is indicated, a *direct speaking to the lost or invading entities is good*, to help them to "clean themselves up" and thus raise their vibration higher so that they are more easily assisted.

The case histories already described sketch the general pattern of the techniques that I have used. There are a few differences in approach when the souls are wandering or when they are obsessing a living person. Professionally I follow this type of therapeutic pattern:

When the client suspects the presence of an invisible energy or wandering entity, I induce her into hypnosis (with her consent, of course, to become the channel) and call the entity—for example, "Grandmother, we are calling you. Are you here? Is it you who is in the bedroom at C's house?" If there is no answer, or if the client's "No" finger rises, I go on, "Then I am calling the entity who is in the bedroom at night, making it cold. Please come and talk to us. C gives her permission for you to use her voice. What is your name?" And so on.

This same approach is used when a "ghost" has been felt at a certain location: "I am calling the entity who is near the hill where the accident occurred in June of last year. Please come and speak with us."

As mentioned numerous times, space and time in the invisible realms are not very important. This channeling may be done at a graveside, as a professor and his wife did when calling the deceased mother, or it may be performed at the therapist's office or at the client's home. The "calling" is the *thought* of the client and the therapist, but the spoken word adds to the power of the call.

Nor is the relationship of the channel to the entity of particular importance unless there is an emotional factor involved, such as fear, grief, love, or dislike. In such cases it is well to ask a different person to be the channel. A parent may be either the very best channel for a child who has died, or the parent may be so emotional that he or she is not capable of the sort of passive, open, impersonal reception necessary. Yet if the person channeling has a personal interest in the situation, that is an asset: a knowledge of the accident, an acquaintance with the family, and so on. Even a total stranger hundreds of miles away from the client may be an excellent channel, however, if willing to be so. For these reasons, "remote" work is not only possible but quite feasible and is performed by an increasing number of therapists. Eugene Maurey and Irene Hickman, D.O., are pioneers in this field. The absent client need not even be aware on the conscious level of this work, but it is ethical to ask, through the channel, if the client's Higher Mind gives permission.

Questions we ask the entity through the channel are the routine ones to learn the sex of the discarnate entity and its age (it ceases aging at death except in rare instances, when it tries to keep up with the flow of the life around it). If we know that this is a small child, a girl, then we know how to talk to her. To the child we may speak comfortingly, asking if she is afraid, and if so, what she is afraid of. If the entity says it is old, a man, we speak to the entity in a different way, asking if he is ill, tired, lonely, etc.

After getting the basic facts about the entity and dispelling any fears, the next step is suggesting the clearing of such negatives as are still remaining, and assuring the entity that it is not necessary to stay in the earth-plane close to anything that was formerly precious or to hide from anything that was formerly feared. We have contacted souls who felt that they had to stay close to their photographs in the Holocaust Memorial, because the photographs represented *themselves*. They were *kept earth-bound by the very memorial meant to honor them!* Cynthia, a sensitive in our group, feels that the Viet Nam Memorial likewise holds earth-bound the minds of many of the persons listed. These persons can be rescued and released, however, by exactly such methods as are described here, one by one, or even in groups, perhaps especially if the individual names are read aloud.

In the case of *obsessing entities* my approach is very similar. I almost routinely now ask a new client's "Yes" or "No" fingers to respond (in hypnosis) to my question, "Is there any mind or consciousness, any entity, in C's body or aura that does not belong to C himself?" The subconscious mind can examine all through C's body and aura in a matter of two or three seconds and respond. If there is no response I assume that an entity is indeed present but does not want to be discovered and will not permit the "Yes" finger to move; nor will the truthful subconscious mind of the client move the "No" finger falsely. I say to the entity, "Don't be afraid of me. I really do want to help you get to a better place."

Having learned that something is in C that "does not belong" to him, the approach is the same as for wandering entities: I ask the entity's name, age, sex, and the circumstances of "the last time you were in your own body—just *see as an observer without pain or fear*, and tell me: What happened?"

There are various other questions that are of interest when speaking to an obsessing entity, but the above are the chief ones. When an idea of the entity and its death has been obtained, I know how to address the problems of the entity first, to enlighten it, encourage it, and direct it safely into the normal pathway to the next stage of its progress. After that, the problems of the *client* are the focus of attention.

The types of obsessing entities include frightened ones and angry ones, meek ones and stubborn ones, and also some that are not human. (These latter are of several types, too, and are only mentioned here. Bill Baldwin, Ph.D., and Irene Hickman, D.O., are among the first contemporary therapists to have written about dark entities that invade living persons. I refer you to their books, my 1986 paper, and my book, *Freeing the Captives.* Please see Bibliography.)

When *mass deaths* occur, we are told by our spiritual advisors not to try to help the people one at a time: "Do not try to be nurses or doctors. In meditation visualize (or describe verbally) an imaged safe road or highway *and call the souls* to come onto the highway. They will be taken care of from there. Remember that these things are known beforehand and preparations are made for those to come over. We miss some, however, and are glad for any help that you on that side can give."

This instruction was offered because one of our group, a nurse with a wonderful talent for astral travel and the ability to assist the dead or dying on the astral level (leaving her physical body asleep at home) had found herself physically exhausted the morning after she had spent the night in her astral body trying to help the many who had been killed in the mudslide in Colombia in 1987. She said that their death had occurred so suddenly while they were sleeping that many souls were still stunned. She attempted to rouse them and get them started toward the Light. She added that a good many were still sleeping under the mud not yet ready to awaken to the new life.

We asked in meditation how we could help such persons without being depleted ourselves, and the answer was as given: "Do not try to be nurses or doctors (trying to help one at a time)." We noted the words, "the souls of those to come over," a confirmation of our feeling that there is a "right time" for most persons to give up the physical body.

And other words struck us, too, confirming what we had been reading from other sources: that these so-called Acts of

God, these "natural disasters" (as we human beings call them) are known beforehand to those on the other side, and preparations have been made to receive the souls of those destined to come.

Those other thoughts, too, caused us to think: that even the high spiritual helpers on the other side may "miss some" souls—perhaps some of those still sleeping or some who refuse to go for various reasons—and therefore even our small human efforts to help are welcomed.

How You Can Help

If you have been reading through the preceding chapters I believe you already have a good idea of how you yourself can help a friend or relative—or an unknown person whose story you have come across in a newspaper or on the television—whose body has died and whose consciousness you think may be in trouble of some kind, or at least unhappy or lonely.

In many cases, the remedy is very simple. First is the brief but very important process of centering yourself, of calming your mind and quieting your feelings of loss, loneliness, grief, etc., before you start trying to help the deceased one. Souls are highly sensitive to the unspoken thoughts and emotions of the living and a false cheerfulness will not fool them a moment.

Therefore *work on yourself first,* talk to your own soul first about the freedom that you desire for your loved one (or your stranger) until you do feel true compassion and a selfless desire to help. Then ask for wisdom, guidance, and protection for yourself and the other souls, embodied or discarnate.

The *second* step is to call the person by name or by location or some other identifying circumstance and explain to the (invisible to you) spirit of the deceased person how its body died and point out that now, although people consider that person dead, the person is still alive, listening to you. Speak tactfully and gently as you would if you could see the person right there with you. Don't merely say, "You're dead!" The point is to convince the soul that although it is still aware and conscious, its body is now dead. It may have not realized this.

If you just talk to your deceased one as if he or she were present right beside you (as indeed the consciousness of that person may well be!), please be very careful *not to let your own emotions drop into your wording terms like "lonely" or "miss you" or "need you."* Remember instead that your purpose is to help, not to drag back nor to weigh down; your purpose is to release and to free and lighten the soul of the deceased one.

It might be wise for you to write out a sketch of what you wish to say to your loved one or to the stranger you want to contact and reread what you have written, to be sure your words will serve to help and not hinder your "client." The rule is simple: "ACCENTUATE THE POSITIVE: ELIMINATE THE NEGATIVE."

If you feel more at ease to start with someone else's words when beginning to talk to the disembodied souls, you may get Fiore's book, *The Unquiet Dead*, or Chaplin's book, *The Bright Light of Death*, and read aloud to the soul you wish to help those pages suggested for home-use by lay persons. Dr. Fiore suggests that perhaps the pages might be taped and you may simply play the tape once or twice a day for a few days. Or you may modify the short programs added at the end of this chapter to suit the person and the situation you are meditating for.

Do you feel as if this is a difficult or dangerous procedure, to try to help that friend who committed suicide, or that relative who died of an overdose of drugs? Or the one who left after a long, drawn-out condition in which his cheery disposition crumbled into a sour, angry state of resentment before death finally came? Or the one who died while drunk, or in a state of "sin"? Really those circumstances are not important for you; you do not have to judge whether the soul is good, bad, or at risk. That is not your task. Your offering is your compassion and your desire to help.

However, if you reread some of the little case histories in earlier chapters here (such as the conversation I had with the tough old gun-slinger in fear of hellfire for being bad) you will get some ideas as to how to suggest that your client can sweep out old pains and weakness, old fatigue, old addictions and mean habits, and so on. Be gentle as you suggest such actions, but repeat the suggestions firmly if you feel it advisable. Listen to your own intuition. You may feel the need to repeat your Rescue words on successive days.

Do not be afraid to start. To let you know how simple and easy it can be, let me tell you about some friends of mine. The man, a professor, and his wife had taken a couple of little courses in hypnosis from me, and I had told them about the workshop I had just had from Dr. Bill Baldwin, on the Releasement of obsessing entities. The professor had been gaining experience as a hypnotist, using his willing wife as his subject, and was eagerly looking forward to learning all he could. Then somehow, after the death of his aged mother, his manner changed. He became gloomy, pessimistic, depressed, quite unlike himself.

It was his wife who began to suspect that perhaps the consciousness of the tired sick old mother had moved into him. And it was the wife who suggested that they go together to the mother's grave and talk to her, explaining that her old worn-out body was now gone, dead, and that *she was alive* and needed to be free of the earth-plane, and free of her son's mind and body, letting him also be free. They did talk to her in this fashion, and the professor's symptoms evaporated. (They wrote and told me all this. There was no return of the old symptoms.)

Actually we know now that it was not necessary for them to have gone to the mother's grave, because in the non-physical realms space is unimportant, but none of us at that time realized quite how easy this process of Rescue and of Releasement can be. This was a case of Releasement, since the mother's consciousness was invading her son. Prayers for the deceased serve the same purpose. The beautiful simple words of Charlene Smith, R.N., to her dying mother are an excellent pattern for dispelling fears. (See Chapter Three on Assisted Transition.)

The *third* step—whether you have used a prayer or have been speaking directly to the minds of your "clients" who have died—is to direct their attention toward the Light and tell them to move toward it and to watch for a welcoming guide who comes to escort them home. This third step is important, for countless souls have told us that they feared to leave the earth-plane or the body they have invaded because they "didn't know where to go." They did not know that the Light would come visibly to receive them, so they did not look for any light—and their *expectation* of dim uncertainty or of darkness provided exactly that (just as an expectation of death-as-a-sleep causes many souls to become torpid after death). Therefore it is important to speak of the Light and its warmth, its welcome, and of the guide who will come. On occasion no guide comes, and if you are not clairvoyant you may not know whether or not a guide has come. Then simply invite "someone who cares about this person" to come, a "high, wise, spiritual being," to be the guide and to escort the soul safely into the Light. This wording provides protection from any mischievous or dark entity from turning up as a "guide."

As with the earlier steps of the program, this third step may need to be repeated a few times, especially if the deceased one still has feelings of unworthiness or "badness." The Light understands all and is more than ready to forgive all with limitless love and compassion (infinitely more than we human beings are usually willing or able to offer). However, the preliminary for this forgiveness is for the soul to be *willing* to rid itself of its old undesirable habits and addictions. This is the first move, made by the soul of its own free will; then comes the Light's instantaneous welcome.

When talking to a relative or friend (or a stranger) who you may feel is lost, unhappy, or otherwise in trouble after death, you might say something like this:

> Sally (or Sammy), I have been thinking of you and sending thoughts for your welfare and peace. You are at the beginning of a new period now, and the old time is past. I am sorry it was so rough for you, but now you can shuck off all the old feelings of anger at your helplessness, your feelings of inferiority and loneliness, and start fresh and new. You realize, don't you, that your body is gone? If you think back—without feeling any fear or pain—you will see what happened, and you will know that your body is no longer of any use to you. Neither are the old habits and addictions that bothered you. Just throw them all away and be rid of them. I think of you now as clean and clear and starting fresh. I am sorry no one realized just how desperate you were. We understand more clearly now, and we send you our thoughts and our concern. Look for the Light, Sally (Sammy), and let it shine away your unhappiness. I am thinking of you now as being surrounded by the Light. . . .

(If the person you have in mind has been really a dark character, you might remind your own self of what a therapist, Dr. Hazel Denning, said one time: "The meaner and nastier a person is, the more he is hurting." That thought may help you to help the mean, nasty persons more easily!)

If it is a loved one or relative you are talking to, you might say something like this:

> Dear Jim (or Betty), I think of you often and am so glad that we knew each other as long as we did. I put your picture on the piano and look at it and smile at it every time I pass by. Sometimes I put a vase of flowers up there beside it, too. I know you are happy now. Don't worry about any of us; we'll work at our life-lessons, just as you did, and make you proud of us. Sure, we miss you here, but we are glad that you are with Grandfather and Grandmother now and are free of those old problems, and we are so grateful that you were one of us this long. In my thoughts I see you strong and healthy, strolling or even running through the fields in the sunshine, or wading in the creek, or just lying in the shade of a tree enjoying the beauty and peace all around you. Not a bad vacation after all you've been through, is it! Or are you busy with other things? Knowing you, I bet you have found interesting things to do already! Whatever they are, dear Jim (Betty), I'm pulling for you. And I'll see you sometime myself. I love you!

(Now if you choose to follow one of these suggested little "programs," just go ahead and start chopping it up and changing words until you make it your own, and then have it at hand to read *after you have centered yourself and quieted your mind and emotions.* Remember that this first step is important, before you begin the conversation with your deceased one.)

8

"WHY ME?"

THIS QUESTION ARISES many times in a life. We wonder why a terrible thing has occurred or an unexpected, lovely, and "undeserved" thing. Some people simply shrug and call these occurrences coincidence or accidents. Others go to the opposite extreme and say flatly, "There are no accidents."

The second statement is based on the belief that a just, divine Plan governs all occurrences that ever happen. Well, overall, that seems to be true. In the short view, however, do we dare to say, "There are no accidents," when faced with a deformed new-born baby, a terribly mutilated war casualty, or starving thousands of helpless persons? If these are not accidents, then what are they?

I heard one time that there is a Jewish rabbi in California who had stated that the Holocaust was deserved by the Jewish people. If the report was true, what more cruel thing could he have said? What more presumptuous thing could be said by any person, Jewish or not? Wasn't that Hitler's attitude almost exactly?

We need to be very careful when our opinions and emotions tend to make us think along such lines. It is a variation of the question, "Why me?" to think or say, "Why those people?"

When I was a freshman at college, I was surprised when our English literature teacher assigned us the Book of Job from the Bible to read for the next day. I reread Job, the story of a rich good man who was tested by the Devil to prove to God that no man can really be true to his religious convictions. The Book of Job—originally written, scholars believe, as a play—was an effort to depict the inner sufferings and questions of afflicted persons, and especially the attempts of friends of the afflicted one to try to comfort him—Job's "comforters," they have been called, sometimes with the quotation marks. It is an age-old question, "Why me? Why my child? Why my beloved? Why my mother, my father, my wife, my husband, my son, my daughter?"

The Book of Job gives no real satisfying answer to those questions except to say that if the afflicted one remains true to a firm conviction of eventual justice and divine love, his afflictions will eventually pass away and he will be rewarded by renewed and even extra earthly wealth and prestige. Many questions remain questions. Life does inexplicable things to us frequently. Perhaps the Prologue and Epilogue of the book were added later, as some believe, to attempt to explain why Job suffered so much. (There was no attempt at an explanation of why his wife had to suffer even more, or why his children and faithful servants were killed off, or why his helpless cattle and camels were destroyed.) The Epilogue seems to be a human attempt to explain the unfinished feeling of the play as written originally, whether or not it was actually lived by a person named Job. Were a human-like God and a human-like Devil really bargaining in a human way for a human soul as in the Prologue and Epilogue?

When a client is in hypnosis, the question "Why?" can be asked, and an answer will be forthcoming from the client's own subconscious or superconscious mind. Many times it is a sobering contact with an event long past, an event which is now bearing its karmic effects and balancing up the score, erasing a debt, allowing the perpetrator of a previous injustice or cruelty to experience how it felt to the victim long ago. This is one fairly common reason, the answer to the "Why?": one which may seem at first glance to be cruel in itself but which often relieves the client, with a new depth of understanding of both his past and the present trouble, giving him new insight and patience. I have witnessed this sort of change over and over in such cases (see examples below).

A second answer to the "Why?" is that the Soul, the Higher Mind, of the client may have made a vow in a previous lifetime or a choice in the Planning Stage before the present birth, or it may have offered to do something that would help its fellowmen without being specific as to what that something might be. When a time arrives for the fulfillment of the vow or an opportunity arrives in which the soul can help its fellow beings greatly, circumstances may be such that these actions incur great suffering or stress, far greater than the Soul could have imagined. An example of each of these will be given below.

Still a third answer to the "Why?" is the less frequent (in my practice) request of a client's Higher Mind in the Planning Stage to have an experience that will teach the soul something new, something valuable not known to the soul before. This, it turns out, may·be a dangerous sort of request, even if spiritually motivated and spiritually intended.

In one case that I remember particularly, it was the answer given to a young woman who had been brutally raped a few years before. It was the answer given by her own mind through her own lips as she lay in hypnosis, reviewing the causes for the rape from the high, impersonal position of her Higher Self. Until this moment she had repeatedly agonized on the conscious level as to "Why?" and the psychological repercussions of that experience had marked her in the ways that a psychologist would expect. Now, however, her attitude toward the experience was changed. With a rueful laugh she admitted, "Well, I asked to have an experience that would teach me something I had not known before—and it sure did. Did I bring it on myself?"

Now this sort of change on the part of the victim does not mean that the rapist was blameless! One thinks of the remark of the Teacher of Galilee, "It needs must be that offenses come, but woe unto him by whom they come."

And I, as therapist and sympathetic listener, asked her Higher Self rather tartly, "Why was it that such a traumatic experience was chosen for the soul's learning process instead of a milder one?"

Again, the answer was impersonal: The soul had made no specific description of the type of new experience desired nor had it stated that there were any limitations as to the type and intensity of trauma that might be involved. As to the rape itself, that was more or less fortuitous, as if circumstances were now favorable for the fulfillment of the soul's request and this happened to be it. The karmic repercussion on the rapist would be a different story entirely, but justice would eventually be served there, and my client apparently had no more connection with her attacker, unless she forged chains of fear and hate. If a child had been conceived from the rape, that, too, would have been a separate story, involving the soul of the child also, probably all three of the persons involved.

As an example of the second answer to "Why?"—i.e., that the soul had asked to be given an opportunity to help fellow men—a poignant case comes to mind:

My client was a young woman whose interest in contacting a past life was that she had occasional flash-backs to Hitler's Germany and she wanted to find out why. (Again that "Why?") In hypnosis she found herself standing with her seven-year-old son in a long line of other women and children, being herded by Nazi guards into two lines, one for the women, the other for children. When it was her turn to face the guard, she stood straight and said, "If he goes, I go." (Afterward she commented that she saw a flash of respect in the eyes of the guard and felt that he would gladly have let both of them pass, except that the other guards would see and ask what he was doing.)

"Both of you, then," said the guard, motioning her into the line of children with her son.

They were herded toward the gas chambers, and as they went, she talked to her son about the good times they had had during his life, the happy times, and about life in general, how wonderful it is. When they neared the gas chamber, however, her little son asked about death, and she began to talk to him about dying and death from her spiritually oriented point of view. Inside the gas chamber, crowded on all sides by the others, she realized that they were quiet, listening as she talked, and she felt that her words were of comfort to them as well as to her own little boy. . . .

How many have come out of a gas chamber to tell their story? Quite a few. Rabbi Gershom (see Bibliography) has been collecting stories of persons now reincarnated after dying in Hitler's Germany, and I have encountered a few others besides this one.

In the case of this young lady, when she sought the reason for her dying in a gas chamber, she found that at the Planning Stage her soul had asked for an opportunity to serve people, to help others. Again, the manner of her assistance seemed to be more or less a happenstance: an opportunity had come, no equivalent one had come earlier; now, by her choice to go with her son, this was the last opportunity and it was truly one that would help others.

Karmic Debts Repaid—The Most Frequent Answer

Many answers to "Why me?" come under this heading. A few chosen more or less at random from my files are represented here, illustrating the wide variation of types of persons and types of symptoms they present.

A second client with a story of Hitler's Germany came to me, interestingly enough, on the same day as the one related above. This time the young woman found herself at term in her pregnancy and in hard labor in a death camp, with Nazi nurses and helpers around the delivery table, waiting for the baby's birth rather than giving her any assistance. When at last the baby was born they took it away out of the room while the mother screamed, "My baby, my baby! Where are they taking it? What are they going to do with it?"

Knowing that I was taking a risk of traumatizing her even more, yet knowing that "knowledge erases karma" (as Dick Sutphen likes to point out), I asked her to let her mind follow the baby and see what happened to it. In anguish she saw that they were using it for a "medical" experiment. "They're torturing it!" she cried.

"Let your mind go back and find out why this helpless newborn little baby has to suffer like this. Without pain or emotion, go back and find the reason, the causes, for its having to suffer."

There was a pause; then, sadly, she said, "I see an overseer in Egypt. He is beating the slaves. He has power over them; he uses that power to have total control over them. He enjoys the feeling of power and the ability to control others."

To the law of karma, the law of universal justice, it is the *soul* that is important, not the age of the body, whether newborn or ancient, whether feeble or immensely strong.

In this case my client also learned, through contacting the Higher Self of the child of her previous life, that the soul of the Egyptian overseer had in other lifetimes learned enough already to be deeply repentant of his former cruelty and arrogance and had asked to be given an opportunity to make up for more of the suffering he had caused in that ancient Egyptian life. We also learned that the experience in the Nazi "hospital" almost completed erasing his karmic debt. With his own forgiveness of the Nazi doctors, he would earn the forgiveness of the last of his former slave victims.

There is no eternal damnation of even the most brutal soul, for every soul is given opportunity time after time, life after life, to undo the evil of former actions. Each is also given free will to use the opportunities or to ignore them.

Another story begins in ancient Egypt, again as an arrogant overseer. My client, an attractive young woman school teacher, lay on the cot in my office saying in a cold voice, "I am beating the slaves to make them work harder. I enjoy beating them."

"Why?" I asked.

"Because they are stupid and slow. They are lazy. They are dirty and ugly."

There was no change in the overseer in that Egyptian lifetime. In the succeeding life the former overseer was born as a female who became a very beautiful woman, who again had power and could have used it to benefit others. But her character was still that of a cold-hearted controller of others, and she used that power to dominate and cruelly exploit others.

In the next life she found herself a male again, this time ugly, crippled, with no chance to exert power over others. This dwarfed, crippled man began to understand how it feels to be ugly, to be considered stupid, to be slow of necessity because of his handicapped limbs. Suffering the stigma of society's attitudes then current toward crippled persons, his character began to change. The old power-lust was still present to some degree, but it was modified so that in the next life, the present one, he was trusted with beauty again, again as a female, and given opportunity to use the talents of leadership in a beneficial way as a teacher in a high school— under an arrogant, domineering principal from whom the soul learned how it feels to persons subject to such an individual.

The teacher had admitted to me (before we knew all this) that she enjoyed teaching but always felt impatient and coldly superior toward pupils who were slow, or fat, or otherwise unattractive to her. And she simply could not like the principal, especially his arrogance.

In hypnosis I took her down some visualized steps into a quiet "sunken garden" (which the subconscious mind usually interprets as the subconsciousness itself), and suggested that as she rested there she would presently notice a living being standing outside the gate. It would come into the garden to a point near her, and then the two would communicate. "I see a bear," she said (and to myself I nodded). (The "living being" is often perceived as an animal and is usually a symbol of the subconscious mind's character.)

"A large bear," she continued.

Having gone through some of the previous lives with her in former sessions, I asked, "Has the bear lost some of its fierceness?"

"Oh, a lot!" she exclaimed.

Then I took up the problem of the irritating principal. I asked her mind to ascend to the Superconscious Level and from that high impersonal state to contact the mind of the principal, "not to invade his privacy, but just enough to enable you to understand him better."

There was a pause; then she said softly, "He comes from a large Spanish-American family. . . . He and his brothers were picked on at school. . . . Now he is trying to prove that he is as good as anybody. . . ." Three short sentences, yet they made a great change in her attitude. Was it the cripple she used to be who resonated to society's attitude toward a person handicapped by social bigotry, "picked on at school"?

This little story has a pleasant ending. At the end of the school year the teacher came to my door to return a book and to report, "I just want you to know that the principal and I got along a lot better. In fact, at the big party that the Parent-Teachers' Association gave last week, he came up to me and told me how glad he was that I had come. I almost hadn't. He had sent every teacher an invitation and a request to come, but I really didn't feel like spending the evening that way. I did decide to go, after all, and was glad because I was the only teacher from our school there! Later the principal wrote me a note saying how much he had enjoyed working with me during the past school year."

She was smiling; her eyes were glowing. It was easy to see that she and the principal had resolved most or all of their previous karma, whatever it might have been. And her "bear," still strong but no longer fierce, was now quite a friendly bear!

A professor friend of mine diagnosed his own situation when his colleagues began to make life very uncomfortable for him by strongly opposing his interest and researches into metaphysical and UFO phenomena. In fact, they were making things so hard for him that he was considering resigning from his position as head of his department. In answer to a sympathetic letter of mine, he told me, "Well, I know that in a former life I was Roman soldier, and I guess I was really the north end of a horse going south! So I am trying to be very gentle and patient this time, because I certainly don't want to go through this again!"

In this life he is a kindly patient man, highly talented in psychic ways. Angered by accusations of "unethical conduct" by members of the department he had served faithfully for twenty-five years, he forced his accusers to clear him, but he finally did resign. He is now free to continue his excellent work among UFO abductees. He also gives remarkable therapy to private clients with the assistance of his highly developed intuitive skills and the help of his Spiritual Advisors.

The Web of Information in Discerning the Answer

As we read back through these stories and others like them we discover that several specific concepts are important:
1. The concept of reincarnation and karmic balancing;
2. The concept of a Soul, a Higher Self, in each person;
3. A Life Review of each life just past;
4. and the concept of a prenatal Planning Stage for the coming incarnation of the soul.

These form the fundamental web on which the answers to our "Why's" will be woven, the answers presented in the form of vividly relived experience of the *causative* events of situations we are seeing in the present life.

As we delve into the past lives for reasons that answer the "Why," the subconscious mind may pick out old forgotten *vows* or *deep resolutions,* such as, "I'll get even with you if it's the last thing I do," or, "You can't get away from me; I'll come back and haunt you." The vow may be a loving one, "I'll never leave you"; "I promise I'll come back." All such vows contain enough force, or contain a word like "forever" or "never," so that the subconscious mind carries the message forward into each succeeding life until the vow is canceled. Each such vow needs to be investigated; it may well hold the answer to a "Why?"

Old forgotten *programmings,* either by one's self or by others, will likewise be carried forward by the faithful but non-discriminating subconscious mind, to produce effects in each succeeding life: "Once a Jew, always a Jew"; "Once a Franciscan, always a Franciscan"; "Once an Indian, always an Indian," and so on. This type of programming begins in pride if self-given or in amusement or even contempt if spoken by others. In either case, if the programming is accepted, it means that the soul has limited itself to lifetimes within the programmed group. Because it is a limitation, it is well to neutralize all such programmings and let the soul have freedom to experience life in other milieus.

Similar programmings concerned with psychological limitations need to be canceled out as well: programmings like, "You are so stupid, you'll never amount to anything." That word *never* is one of the most dangerous in the English language. If the subconsciousness of the person *accepts* that image of herself as "stupid," she may very well be limited in intelligence life after life until she manages to destroy the power of that old programming. She herself may have pro-grammed herself so: "I guess I'll always be clumsy"; "Nobody will ever love me"; "Other people have happiness; I never will." Do you notice all those words, "always," "nobody ever will," "never"?

Very similar is the condition in which *curses* and *spells* operate to shadow a life. A curse need not be produced by any black magic or satanic ritual; it may be laid upon another person simply by a strong negative desire that harm come to the person targeted, perhaps with a concrete thought-form of the type of harm wished on that person, perhaps only a nebulous hate or anger. Such ill-will may follow and blight a life for years or even lifetimes, especially if sent forth with the vow of "forever."

The *Review* of the lives past offers the conscious mind the insights of the evaluations and judgments of the *Higher Self* at the superconscious level. There may be a wrenching honesty, a clear impersonal wisdom such as is not obtainable from the conscious level with its "I have figured out" type of reasoning. From the superconscious level the Higher Self speaks with calm, non-judgmental judgment—that is, without anger or criticism, without defensiveness, yet with impartial clarity of vision, revealing what the failures of the life just past have been, what the spiritual successes, and what lessons still need to be worked on in coming lifetimes, and *why*.

During the *interlife*, the period between the death in one earth-life and the birth into the next, the soul is working on the lessons pin-pointed by the last Review so that it is continuing to mature and becoming stronger for the coming incarnated life. Thus, when the soul arrives at the Planning Stage for a new entrance into earthlife, it is clearer and stronger (in spiritual ways) than it was before. The Higher Self will have some suggestions and ideas of its own as to what it feels the coming earth-life needs to include and the things it wants and hopes for.

Wise discarnate Counselors also offer thoughts and suggestions in the *Planning Stage* and sometimes are quite insistent on certain types of experiences that they know this particular soul needs for its spiritual advancement—experiences that the (lower) soul would most gladly avoid if at all possible. Some persons (in hypnotic regression to the Planning Stage) admit that they were all but forced into birth again and entered earth-life "kicking and screaming"—and they did not mean only physically—they meant emotionally!

Each soul does have free will. However, as Lord Dowding of London remarked, sometimes it seems as if one's free will is rather forcibly bent by the advice of the Higher Advisors!

We remember that *karma* includes both dark and bright sides. When a soul at the Planning Stage is selecting karmic lessons to work on in the coming earth-life, it chooses not only some of the weaknesses but also some of the talents, so that the weaknesses decrease and gradually become strengths and the talents mature and become more polished and beautiful. It is not possible for a soul to undertake to balance up all of its karma in one lifetime. Some of the joys are selected to enjoy further; relationships with loved ones are chosen to be renewed and enlarged. Generosities in the past may lead to unanticipated rewards in the coming life. These things will be seen in the Planning Stage by the soul. They will all be forgotten on the *conscious* level very shortly after the soul enters earthlife.

An illuminating example of Planning Stage choice is a case reported by Dr. Bill Baldwin, who was conversing with an entity, a very angry man, who had been obsessing a young woman. The man said that she had hit him with her car and killed him, and he was furious at all women drivers but especially this woman, whom he had tried to attack after his death, and, failing to make any impression physically, had moved in and obsessed her. He felt that she had destroyed his future success and he was very bitter toward her.

Instructed to go to the Planning Stage before his birth into that life, he found that he had been offered several possible times in which he might choose to leave that incarnation: first, at about nine, after a tonsillectomy, or in his teens, from a drug overdose, or at thirty-five he might be hit by a car, or at fifty-two he might have a heart attack, or he might live well into old age and die of a degenerative condition. When Baldwin asked which of these possible deaths he thought would be preferable, the man decided that he would prefer to leave his body at about thirty-five, while he was in good health and happy with the prospect of a good career ahead. Then, thoughtfully, he began to sense that in an earlier life he had killed this woman in the prime of her life. His choice of dying at the prime of his present life was a karmic balancing, and the woman was unknowingly fulfilling his own wish when her car swung around a corner just as the man stepped absentmindedly into the street from the curb and into her way.

Baldwin said that the man "understood that it had been his own choice. She was never to blame. He had wasted many earth-years in his anger. The impact of this was devastating and liberating at the same time."

The subconscious mind does not forget. In its *memory bank* repose all the former vows, resolutions, fears, angers, talents, and loves of all the previous lifetimes. It is this package, this condensed seed or kernel, its personal *Predispositions*, with which a baby is born into the world.

> "Not in entire forgetfulness
> And not in utter nakedness
> But trailing clouds of glory do we come
> From God who is our home,"

wrote the poet Wordsworth in the last century, in his "Ode on Intimations of Immortality."

It is the soul itself by its thoughts, words, and actions during its earth lives that determines whether we come trailing clouds of glory or are pushed into earth-life kicking and screaming, reluctant to begin facing up to and dealing with the harsh results of our former negative life habits.

The fine part is that there are always opportunities to change, to improve. *Always.* There is no such thing as hopelessness in a soul's situation. There is no such thing as eternal condemnation. Nor is there such a thing as perennial "salvation" in the sense of simply relaxing in a heaven or Happy Hunting Ground of some type and letting the universe and all its activities and problems go by. We are told that there is eternal progress, eternal unfoldment, and eternal embrace by the all-embracing Love and Wisdom.

So, when I wonder *Why* this or that "terrible disaster" occurs, although I do respond with human emotions, I can still my emotions and contact a higher level and wait for a deeper, higher, more impersonal spiritual meaning that answers the "Why?" Usually I can find the answer quickly if I work with a friend and one of us goes into hypnosis and from there to a High Level to inquire. Meditation alone is not always high enough for me to achieve such a contact by myself, nor is prayer. Other persons have had such a contact through a spontaneous Near-Death Experience or a mystical experience. Even one single contact of this sort eases the mind, giving a profound sense of trust in the Plan of Life.

When my sons were in high school, one of them came home from school one day and greeted me cheerfully, "Mom, is there justice in the universe?" (An ordinary question from a teenage boy to his mother, I suppose.)

With equal cheerfulness, I said, "No," and we both laughed.

Then I added seriously, "Not in the short run, son, but in the long run, yes, I am convinced that there is justice."

That was before I began working regularly with clients whose past-life sequences revealed again and again that:

- what a person sows is what he or she eventually reaps;
- what a person gives is what he gets back;
- love begets love; hate begets hate;
- what is good breeds good; what is evil breeds evil.

All the great teachers have taught these things.

There is much evidence of firm justice in the universe, but not punitive in attitude—simply that what we do to or for others will rebound to ourselves in due time, for joy or for pain. We can choose what is to be in our future by the way we live in the present. Karma does not punish; it is like the law of gravity: impersonal, all-pervading, impartial, most of the time beneficial—but it is up to us to choose where we step lest we walk off a cliff!

It is tragic that this reap-what-we-sow Law of Life has fallen into disregard and that many people have never heard of it. It is tragic that many who heard it in childhood now consider it childish and ignore it. "Do unto others as you would like them to do unto you," says the Golden Rule. These days I have heard it quoted (misquoted) as "Do onto others before they do onto you." It was meant at first as a joke, but children who heard adults saying it thought it really was the Golden Rule!

More than 500 years B.C.E. the young prince of the Gautama clan in India left his palaces and went afoot and alone into the world to seek answers to the "Whys." He had suddenly become aware of the suffering, the sickness, the aging, and dying of people and had been told that these could not be prevented. He felt sure that somehow they could be, and he went out to seek the answers.

Years later, after his Enlightenment, he had to admit that there was a certain irreducible amount of pain—pain due merely to the fact of physical existence on a physical earth in physical bodies. (Scientists might say it is because nerves are necessary in order for a living body to contact the environment, and sometimes the contact is unduly sharp or harsh, and the nerves cry, "Pain!" In this manner, nerves and pain are a protection.)

The Newly Enlightened One, however, found that most pain in human beings is due to emotions—to selfish desires that cannot be entirely fulfilled or to aversions toward undesired things that cannot be avoided. He also came to see clearly that a certain deed or thought or motive in the present is a cause which will produce a definite effect in the future. "So live that you will not have to suffer remorse," he told people. In a similar admonition he phrased it as, "Do not unto others as you would not have them do unto you."

He had found the keys to the elimination of suffering, and they turned out to be keys that must be used by each person individually. He could describe and offer the keys, but each person has to accept and use them for himself or for herself.

9

NATURE'S
STERN WISE MERCY

Why Death Anyway? The Balance of Nature

THERE WAS A MOVIE LONG AGO called *Death Takes a Holiday*, in which Death, portrayed as a mild, pleasant man, came to earth in that guise to find out why people feared Death so much. Because he was now in a human body and therefore was not on the job in his real position as Death, he was taking a holiday. Of course that meant that nothing could die until he returned from his vacation. Many incredible "escapes" occurred to people during Death's vacation. Amazing feats of foolhardy daring were performed. Besides, sometimes the inability of a person to die made complications for those who would be survivors. The movie was a comedy, well thought out and well performed and with an unmistakable meaning: Death is as necessary to Life as birth is.

In the Hindu religion one of the three Aspects of God is Shiva, the Destroyer-Regenerator (the others being the Creator, Brahma, and the Sustainer, Vishnu). Shiva has the dual role of destroying old, deformed, injured, and outworn forms and taking the life of those bodies to place into new, fresh forms and regenerate them. One of Shiva's aspects is the Divine Dancer, Nataraja, who balances delicately on the toes of one foot which rests on a demon and subdues it. He gestures gracefully with his four arms: one holding a tiny drum to symbolize life; one holding a little fire, symbolizing the burning ghat of death; one sweeping things away; and the fourth one extended in blessing. (There are other interpretations of the last two arms.) As Nataraja, Life and Death and Regeneration dance over the world maintaining a graceful balance while moving from point to point in the Dance.

In biology this is called the Balance of Nature. In college biology courses my professors repeatedly and matter-of-factly spoke of the various ways in which Nature, when unbalanced in any manner, works to restore balance throughout the whole.

We were also told what the effects would be if any species of living creature were to reproduce at its present rate and none of the offspring were to die. Plant lice, reproducing at their normal rate, would overwhelm the land, for instance. Termites—plants of any certain species—bacteria of one kind or another—all of these would outgrow any usefulness to themselves or to other creatures, filling the earth but starving.

There are many examples of this type of overgrowth, although Death did not take a complete holiday in these cases; it was only that the natural predators of the species were absent or nearly so:

- the rabbit plague in Australia after rabbits were introduced;
- the plague of prickly pear cactus in Australia;
- the rapid spread of English sparrows in the New World after homesick English immigrants and sailors introduced them;
- the more recent introduction of starlings and their swift spread across the country; and so on.

Prey and Predators—The Food Chain

Half a century ago the word "predator" almost always had a very negative connotation, and to call a person "predacious" was a derogatory comment on the person's life-style. For that matter, when applied to a human being, that still is true. When applied to natural relationships, however, the word "predator" is now used as calmly as the word "prey" and a balance between the two is implied.

I used to think of writing a little story or parable of a time when the gods were young and had been given power to create life-forms on the new planet. Each young, enthusiastic god, with helpers as needed, might select a certain field in which to specialize: Each god might choose a pattern ("Phylum") different from the others, a pattern to develop and evolve into many types of forms. All patterns and variations needed to remain in Balance, as the Great Plan required.

With the creation of living physical forms, however, came the need to manage somehow that the forms—at first very simple, just one cell each—could nourish more efficiently their life-activities such as movement, growth, and so on. They needed to take in substances that could be called "food." Chemicals dissolved in the sea-water and ooze? Yes. But more was needed to sustain the life-energies and allow the living creatures to reproduce faster and become more complex—"Morsels" of some nutritious substance. The gods began to plan how to create enough such Morsels.

Then one young god might have suggested boldly, *"Life for the Morsels!"* and astonished the other gods, who probably were ready to veto such a thought, perceiving that some of their own pet creations might come to be considered Morsels and thus be taken out of manifestation.

As the conversation turned into argument and then into discussion, however, the gods began to consider the plan seriously, especially in view of the undeniable fact that the Great Plan of the First Creator called for the conservation of Energy, even though Energy might be changed from one form into another. If the new little simple creatures were to be able to evolve, Morsels of something nutritious were needed for their nourishment. And if so, then would it not be of value to the Morsels to allow them, also, to reproduce and enjoy Life, at least until they were needed as Morsels?

Yes, agreed the gods, but what if the Morsels forgot their primary function, to be Morsels, and began to want to keep the Life and exist for themselves?

"If I were a Morsel and had Life, I'd want to keep living," proclaimed one god. Then an older god suggested thoughtfully, "Suppose we make Life and Living their Primary functions and they become Morsels only when need arises for another creature?"

Perhaps that is where the argument still remains, as the sequence now called the Food Chain. And *Homo* believes that his species is at the very top of the Food Chain, right? It is so only when a person has had the body embalmed and planted deeply. Otherwise, in the natural Order of Things, the human body, once at the top of the Food Chain, now becomes nutriment for the life-forms at the very bottom of the Food Chain, the bacteria of decay. But that's all right. It is all in the Order of Things, in the Balance of Nature.

Nature Restores Balance

When I was a medical student, our professors accepted calmly the concept of the Balance of Nature. One of them told us that if, during our lifetimes, the scientific community should feel triumphant over any particular type of disease— for instance small pox—we as doctors should not allow ourselves to become too confident, because Nature would take care that the causative agent of small pox would gradually develop immunity to any type of preventive or killing treatment that human beings might devise. I thought of this when the medical world began to boast that poliomyelitis has become a thing of the past; that tuberculosis has been controlled and all but wiped out; that the threat of measles is no more. Nature takes care of her own, and the "causative agents" of these diseases are living things, not merely chemical toxins or pollutants.

During the forties and fifties in our country home I noticed that each season there seemed to be a tremendous overpopulation of some *one* species of insect or arachnid. One spring black crickets would be everywhere, inside the house as well as outside. The next year the black cricket population would be back to normal, but little house spiders would take over, or daddy-long legs, or white crickets, or wasps.

Each year after the population explosion of that species, the number observable seemed to be back to the usual. I did a lot of thinking, because now we see that it is the species of *Homo sapiens*, the human race, overpopulating wildly.

Dr. Frank Laubach (the founder of Laubach Literacy) told us a thought provoking true story back in the 1950s. He told of a well-known American philanthropist who asked his lawyer what he should do with his money. "I don't want to face my Maker with all these millions," he said.

The lawyer recommended starting new little clinics and hospitals in many poor countries. The philanthropist did so and had them staffed with health workers who in turn taught the local people first of all how to use aseptic techniques when a baby was born.

"So the babies' umbilical cords were no longer tied off with an old shoestring for luck, nor cut with the father's dirty knife for strength, and the babies no longer got tetanus of the newborn. They lived, they became teenagers, they began having babies of their own. It is now thirty years later, and there are *more hungry people* in the world than ever." He spread his hands. "What started as a truly philanthropic enterprise turned out to cause more suffering and starvation than before. I don't know what the answer is."

I could not help feeling depressed back then in the 1950s when I contemplated the coming decades. I foresaw that Nature might create resistant strains of bacteria to the modern "miracle drugs" and that epidemics of "new" diseases might be one of her instruments to control the overgrowth of the human species. I foresaw floods and fires resulting from the erosion of mountains stripped of trees and prairies plowed up for fields. I did not realize what profound changes in the weather might occur nor did I expect so many more political and military uprisings, nor the wholesale sex-drive all over the world plus the reduction in infant mortality that have been shooting the earth's population up toward asymptote, as the graph sweeps up toward a frightening vertical line. This last tendency cannot be controlled even by contraceptives and wholesale abortion nor by many wars.

Laubach spoke in 1955. This is now 2000, another forty-five years, and look at the millions who are starving or barely able to subsist as they swarm over the denuded earth like plant-lice (except in a few countries like ours which temporarily still have space).

An article by Richard V. Lee, M.D., was published (1994) in *The Pharos* medical magazine, from which I'd like to quote:

> Good health is a matter of harmony: a balance between a variety of opposing dualities. . . . Bad health has probably

contributed more to the evolution of *Homo sapiens* than any of us care to admit. Sickness and health are ecologic necessities.

Without death there is no equilibrium, no room for young and new creatures, and no return of biologic essentials to the environment. . . .

One of the features of modern medicine is the postponement of dying. . . . The notion that cancers are composed of cells that refuse to die is intuitively sensible. Human populations composed of increasing numbers of individuals who refuse to die may be similar to neoplasia, producing environmental cachexia (emaciation and weakness) and ultimately death.

Disease and death have influenced individual and communal destiny more often than physicians care to recognize. Great plagues have swept through human populations for time out of mind. They have been agents of biologic and cultural evolution, and eradicating them may have unforeseen consequences for the health and the future of the human species.

Now these are not the brash conclusions of a youthful doctor whose hobby is arm-chair philosophizing. These are the scientific conclusions of a professor of medicine, pediatrics, and obstetrics after twenty years of studies in four geographically isolated agriculturally marginal areas: Kashmir, Ladakh, Kenya, and central Brazil. The studies "illustrate the fragile equilibrium between the human population, with its pastoral and/or agricultural activities, and the environment."

As a physician in a prestigious position at the State University of New York at Buffalo, Dr. Lee is daring to say what a good many other doctors and anthropologists may have been thinking secretly.

We do not like these thoughts. We deny their accuracy. We want to get rid of them. And it may be true that Dr. Lee has overstated some points: it may be that population control can be achieved in other ways than by Nature's methods, which include disease and starvation.

There is a tribe that inhabits an island in the South Seas where the population controls itself by the number of coconuts available for food on the island. It is reported that when the coconut crop is good, more babies are conceived than during periods when the coconut harvest is small. This type of breeding control is reminiscent of that of birds, many species of which do not mate and lay eggs if there are no places for nests to be constructed.

On television there was a documentary about an African tribe in which each newly married couple took two or three years becoming acquainted with each other and with the activities of the tribe as adult members before beginning to copulate and prepare for parenthood. I still remember the blank expression on the anthropologist's face as he related this (to him incredible) tribal habit. The tribe easily controlled its population simply by controlling its mating habits. The tribe had not been programmed from early childhood that the sex urge is constant and uncontrollable, and had evolved its own rhythms and attitudes appropriate to its environment and life style and the availability of food.

When the environment, including adequate habitat for nests or homes, is allowed to control population, disease need not be a *necessary* agent of control. In this I tend to disagree with Dr. Lee. Still, he may be right.

The pollution of the oceans may be as serious a death-producing condition as overpopulation. I wish to quote from a letter (8-22-95) from Captain Jacques-Yves Cousteau:

> Reefs that teemed with life only 10 years ago are almost barren!

... it is our duty and responsibility to do more than ever before to educate the world over about the delicate linkages of life. *The problems of the sea simply cannot be separated from those of the rest of the planet. All life is connected—and the great life-giving bank is the sea.*

But ... if the sea continues to be used as a global sewer, if we continue to disrupt the natural processes of our biosphere, we will surely bring upon ourselves catastrophe after catastrophe.

We must *never* let this happen!

I believe that if enough of us care, if enough of us are willing to battle against the forces of destruction, we *can* prevent such catastrophes from ever happening.

A cartoon stays in my mind: A man is standing by a little booth beside an open field; a sign by the booth offers "Land for Sale"; in the distance a nuclear reactor's shape looms against the sky. Looking from the sign to the reactor in the distance the man asks the realtor, "What is the mortality rate around here?" The land-seller replies, "Same as everywhere else—one per person."

One death per person *is* the normal rate, isn't it. But when ten or a hundred, or a hundred thousand at one time meet death, we feel a far greater impact.

An attitude similar to that of the land-seller was expressed by Dr. Harlow Shapley, the famous astronomer, whom I heard in New Orleans years ago. He said that a woman in a previous audience had asked, "Is it true that man is able now to blow up the whole earth?"

"Oh, yes," replied the lecturer casually, "but it isn't as if the earth were a *major* planet."

That is the attitude the solar system itself takes. It is the attitude of the earth toward us: "Could I cause the human race to become extinct? Oh, yes; but it is not as if the extinction of any species, even the human race, would be a *major* loss. I could replace any species with a newer, better one."

Mass Extinctions and Biological Evolution

Since the Great Comet Crash of 1994, when the fragments of Shoemaker-Levy 9 plunged into Jupiter, watched by untold numbers of earthlings peering through telescopes, the general public has been aware that such cosmic events really do happen in our lifetimes. Craters on the moon and other celestial bodies, or even the scars of such events on our earth, seem to be rather removed from our day-today reality: interesting, but not as important as our schedule for the day.

Back in 1933 a novel was published as a serial in the *Rocky Mountain News* about such an event occurring to the earth. I was fascinated by the tale and cut out the pages each Sunday and saved them. Many years later I realized that the story had become one of the early classics of science fiction: *When Worlds Collide* by Balmer and Wylie.

The plot in brief was that astronomers in South Africa had discovered a distant pair of great bodies, a double planet, approaching the earth on a collision course. They sent the information by special courier to fellow astronomers in England and America. When the date of the future collision had been carefully calculated, the first problem for the scientists was whether to tell what they knew, and to whom. What would be the reaction of the public? At least they must tell the President and Britain's leaders, and all other astronomers. After that they determined to build a space ship for a carefully selected number of healthy intelligent individuals each with special knowledge or talents, a ship that might take them and a store of earth-seeds, plant-cuttings, and useful animals to a new home on the larger planet, leaving the Earth and the smaller planet to destroy each other. Their plan became rumored among the public, however, and in the last days before the scheduled lift-off, the compound was stormed by frantic people trying to get in.

The story ends with a successful lift-off of the ship and a successful landing on the passing planet, to face a new and unknown type of existence.

Almost as drastic an event as the one portrayed in the story was the event that exterminated the dinosaurs and a multitude of other species at the end of the Cretaceous Era. The full story of this event has been discovered in stages and only during the past twenty years have the various pieces come together to form a nearly complete description of what happened:

Sixty-five million years ago, when huge dinosaurs were abundant, a large chunk of rocky material, a small asteroid about ten kilometers in diameter, smashed into the Gulf of Mexico where the Yucatan Peninsula now is. Scientists had known that the rock deep under this region was fractured; in 1991 they discovered that this area was an enormous crater (which was named Chicxulub). An article in *Astronomy* magazine for October 1995 ("Target Earth" by David Morrison) states:

> Scientists now estimate from the crater's size that the progenitor asteroid hit with an astounding energy equivalent to more than five billion Hiroshima atomic bombs (100 million megatons).
>
> Aside from the immediate effects of heat and concussion, two major post-impact events did the dinosaurs in: a firestorm followed by excessive cold. . . . [L]arge quantities of rock and dust [were] blown out from the crater. When this ejecta rained down . . . it produced a meteor shower of almost unbelievable proportions. Meteors turned the sky red-hot and ignited terrestrial forests and grasslands. Telltale soot from this firestorm is found in sediments from the K/T boundary [Cretaceous/Tertiary] at sites all over the world. Most land animals probably perished by fire.
>
> Then came the cold. . .

. . . a sizable portion [of the material blown out of the crater] remained suspended in the atmosphere for months, blocking photosynthesis and plummeting temperatures on the dark surface beneath the clouds.

Suppression of photosynthesis lead to a breakdown in the ocean food chain that killed most marine creatures. Survivors had to hunker down to a global drop in temperature not unlike the 'nuclear winter' scenario postulated during the later days of the Cold War. . . . It was the thermal pulse from reentering ejecta and the subsequent darkness caused by suspended stratospheric dust that did most of the killing. . . .

Luis and Walter Alvarez of the University of California at Berkeley have proposed that similar events may have accounted for other mass extinctions that are known by the fossil record in geologic history. Moreover, the Alvarezes suggest that such *major disturbances of the Balance of Nature may have given a tremendous stimulus to biological evolution,* spurring Nature to spawn a multitude of new creatures from the remnants of the various species which survived the great changes. In this sense, mass extinctions could actually be considered the *assistants of Nature,* clearing away the scenery and the actors of one scene so that she can start anew with different scenery and new characters that she fashions from the old ones that were not swept away, dressing them in fresh forms and in new beauty. Whether such changes of scenery are fortuitous or whether Nature or Destiny or God has a program for the Earth that includes these vast events I do not know. Did the little asteroid "have Earth's name on it?"

Will there be another one with the Earth's name on it? A much smaller one struck Tunguska, Siberia, in 1908, a bolide of about fifteen megatons. In this desolate region more than two thousand square kilometers of forest were devastated. Few people were killed, but the report of the enormous event gradually spread and a scientific expedition was sent to the region seventeen years afterward. Meteor Crater in Arizona was formed by a meteorite of similar energy, fifteen megatons. These visitors from space do strike Earth now and then, even within our lifetimes.

As you have read this chapter have you noticed it is mostly about the death of bodies (of dinosaurs or people) without the mention of souls? It is the familiar way in which we usually do think of such fatal events as these: *fatal*, destined by Fate, which in this sense we make synonymous with *mortal*.

Summing up before we go back to the souls: We have done our Earth much harm with our poisons, our bombs, our pollutants, and most especially with our radioactive substances. Plutonium burns the Earth most and will continue to hurt her for hundreds of thousands of years. The repeated shocks from nuclear bombs have jarred and jolted her body and have upset her systems. And the floods of hate, the outbursting volcanoes of rage, the cruelties and viciousness, the greeds, the terrors, the despairs—all these have fouled and sickened her astral body.

The Earth is crying; she is ill; she burns with fever in some places; she weeps floods of tears in others; she shivers with chills; she erupts with boils. It is time for her to cleanse herself and gradually restore herself to health and beauty once more.

In the cleansing process the Earth may end by establishing a different new balance in which many of her present species have been allowed to die out. We know that already many species are becoming extinct every week. I do not think the human race will become extinct but Nature may sternly call us to account for all the harm we have done to her and pare our numbers down to what she finds is a reasonable level. I find it a very sobering thought. We are some of her children, but to her we are no more important than termites, bluebirds, or dolphins.

How Do We Meet the Crisis?

So, as a lesson in finding out how much we have learned about Death (of the bodies) and Life (of the souls), let us suppose that our astronomers discover that one of the asteroids which has previously passed Earth as a "near miss" of some three million miles is in an orbit that will come perilously close on its next revolution around the sun, in let's say five years. It may even sideswipe the Earth, jarring her out of her orbit to some degree. There will undoubtedly be horrendous disturbances of our weather patterns and ocean currents; there will undoubtedly be terrific earthquakes as the gravity of the oncoming body affects the Earth's crust. We ask, "Will there be much loss of life?" And we dread to hear the answer.

I asked that same question of one of my clients when she was in progression hypnosis and saw in the future the coast of China unrecognizably distorted. I asked her to go back to the time when the coastline changed and report on what was happening. She saw a terrific storm, a typhoon, moving up the coast.

"Is there much loss of life?" I asked. My wording was just what a doctor might well use, but they were earth terms, as her reply pointed out to me:

"I see," she said quietly, "many souls rising up."

That attitude is exactly what we need to develop in ourselves. Jews and Christians who are sincerely comforted by their religious tenets will say, "Our times are in His hands," and "Underneath are the Everlasting Arms." They will face the oncoming events with courage and faith, even if perhaps with some human dread. They will face the deaths of their bodies in the same spirit.

Some people may hold the attitude of the medieval monk in the legend: When he was asked what he would do if he knew that the world was going to come to an end at four o'clock the next afternoon he said, "Four o'clock? I'll be working in my garden."

Muslims who are sincere in their trust of Allah as the One God will say, "As God wills; it is the will of Allah."

But in the heart of each human being during a crisis there will be a testing of "beliefs" and of "faith," whether or not the person holds any certain religious belief or not. Each is contemplating his own death, no longer as a matter of sometime but as a matter of soon.

There will be some who react as the hordes did in the story of the colliding worlds, losing all self-restraint, giving way to panic, trying to snatch what safety they can find at the expense of any who get in their way, reverting to animal terror. These may give up all sense of humanness and become swayed by reactions of self-preservation. Others may wildly try to seize the pleasure of each moment; the "Eat, drink, and be merry for tomorrow we die" attitude.

And there may be some who philosophically take time to think seriously about what death means and what their own mental and emotional reactions to their imminent demise is. Happy are those who can come to the conclusion that only the body will die, only the body will suffer the great Extinction. Life will continue, thought will persist, and stresses and pains of physical life will be replaced by the freedom and light, the joy and laughter that are reported by so many souls who have left their physical vehicles in death.

There may even be a number of a more mental type who respond to the coming disruptions with an impersonal but keen sort of fascination, an intense interest in the entire process of this vast Change, knowing that it is such as occurs only once in many millions of years, ending one Era and allowing a new one to begin, whether by cataclysmic geo-physical disturbances or by sweeping epidemics or climatic changes. These persons feel they are permitted to see and feel the *Old* ending and the *New* being prepared for.

These types of responses may overlap, of course, or else alternate in the same individual. Which type are we? are you?

Several books have been published in the past few years about such a coming Great Change. Intimations have been given to some of my clients who have contacted the future in their hypnotic sessions as did the woman mentioned. We are instructed not to dread the coming changes, just to continue "working in our gardens" and clearing up our own lives, preparing our own souls for the changes. These *spiritual* things are what are most important for us all to be doing. Death of the body is still inevitable, and still "only one per person."

Driving along a highway in southwestern Colorado a few years ago, admiring the beauty of mountains, valleys, forests, sky and clouds, I found myself yearning for it to remain just as it was. "All this beauty, all this loveliness could be wiped out or changed past recognition. . . . How sad that would be, what a waste. . . ."

And then suddenly it struck me how presumptuous was my idea that Nature, who had spent hundreds of millions of years producing this beauty, could not produce just as much beauty or even more after clearing the scenes of the present beauty! My little human mind could not believe in Nature's *continuing* plan and power. I had to laugh aloud at myself. After all the courses I have had, studying the works of Nature in plant and animal life and in human development, I was still doubting her beauty of plan even while admiring the loveliness of the forms she had evolved! The laughter helped me, even though at times I still feel some nostalgia as if I am halfway in a changed future already. Nevertheless, I am working in my garden as faithfully as possible.

Nature's Stern Impartiality

Now at last we get back to the surviving souls of the dying bodies. If it is dinosaurs and trilobites whose bodies have been swept away by the events of time, disease, and cataclysms, I venture to say it was not because those creatures had "sinned." If we human beings experience mass deaths in floods, in droughts, in earthquakes, or in epidemics in various places around the world, I cannot agree with any who judgmentally pronounce that these stricken persons have "deserved" such a death because of some lack or sin or neglected ritual.

Nevertheless, if we search deeply for the reason for these great miseries and their consequent release of many souls, we sometimes discover that a cause was a group action in some past time. A good many innocent individuals may get caught up in *group karma*, the karmic working-out of actions perpetrated in a past time by the majority involved now in the group experiences.

Other mass dyings seem to be simply the on-going motion of a natural process. In the fall of the year, for instance, there is always a mass dying or mass slaughter of drone bees and of many worker bees, including, in domesticated bees, those workers who sting to death the drones, for each worker can sting only one time and then die. This, I used to think, was the D-day of the bees, the Death Day. It was necessary to reduce the number of bees that could live through the long winter months in a crowded hive. (Has the Earth become our crowded hive?)

Still other great natural changes are found to be the results of natural forces working on a hemispheric or global scale. Examples are the ocean current of El Niño, the volcanic eruptions around the Pacific Ring of Fire, and the earth-quakes due to plate tectonic movements. These all seem to be part of the Earth's own physiological processes, some of them affected by human intervention, it is true, but perhaps by "sin" only in an environmental sense.

Nature's Mercy

When a mass death is sudden, Nature provides a type of *analgesia, a deadening to pain,* almost an anesthesia that allows movement but numbs the senses and the emotions. In the immediate aftermath of the explosion of the atomic bombs over Japan, those who lived told of seeing silent groups of mortally burned victims staggering toward the river or simply wandering aimlessly. This *emotional numbness* is akin to profound shock. It is a blessing that in crises prevents un-bearable pain and excruciating emotional reactions at least temporarily.

When people have a few moments of forewarning of imminent sudden death, as in a sinking ship or an airplane falling out of control, the consciousness of the ones who know that "this is it" *may withdraw from the body before the body dies,* as mentioned earlier. The foreknowledge of death is a help to the souls in that they are aware that they are about to lose their bodies and when they find themselves still conscious, know that they are free to go on to the "next world."

In individual deaths a similar numbing may occur. For instance, an Alpine guide reported that when he made a misstep and fell many hundred feet down a mountain cliff, he felt only a moderate amount of fear and no panic while falling, whereas later when he saw a friend fall, his own fear and distress were far greater. Most of my clients who re-experienced a fatal fall in a past life reported a calmness that seemed totally inappropriate, or they withdrew from the body and watched it falling as if it were an object unrelated to themselves. This type of reaction occurred in several different cases. It seems to be one of Nature's ways of assisting the transition of the soul from incarnate to discarnate with the greatest ease and smoothness possible.

I read that in the journal kept by Dr. Livingstone (of Livingstone and Stanley fame) he wrote that one time he was attacked and carried off by a large lion, but, although aware of the life-threatening situation and also aware of pain in his shoulder, he felt calm and almost serene. It was the shouts and the counterattack of his black bodyguard that caused the lion to drop him and allowed him to live to tell the story. (I wish I could remember where I found this anecdote.)

If the death is approaching more slowly, whether during an epidemic or after a long disease or a severe injury, Nature arranges another compassionate sequence of physiological events that actually hasten the death and shorten the pre-death period of pain and weakness: the body begins to provide *positive feedback* to the physiological processes. Instead of trying to maintain a state of equilibrium, nature begins to increase and exacerbate each abnormal condition: if the blood pressure falls, there is now a tendency for it to fall still lower; if there is a fever, there is now a spiraling tendency for the temperature to go still higher; if the kidneys are failing, they may now shut down entirely. This type of reverse response is distressing to the nurse or doctor who has been trained to block the worsening of any abnormal condition and bring back homeostasis, the equilibrium of a normal body. Yet when the body has come to the end of its usefulness, Nature provides this way of helping it to die and release the soul.

A patient may unconsciously desire to cooperate with this terminal sequence and be considered by his care-givers to be stubborn and uncooperative. My father-in-law, for instance, complained to me in the nursing home, "They keep forcing me to eat, they keep pushing food at me. I don't like to feel full!" The nurses did their duty and kept him alive; he was able to be moved to his daughter's home, where she cared for him during the remaining months of his life. He was bedfast, irritable, hard to deal with, and his daughter wore herself out attempting to keep him hallway contented. . . . I have wondered if he was not wiser than the nurses who kept forcing him to eat when he did not want to feel full. Those last months of his life were not pleasant for him nor for his daughter. Perhaps Nature had arranged for him to leave his helpless old body sooner but was prevented by the well-intentioned ministrations of his caregivers. In the old days he might have been allowed to use up all his remaining body-fat and energy and quietly leave.

In medical school we students were instructed to write specific directions on a patient's chart in case of incurable and distressing conditions. If the patient was a terminal adult or child, such a directive might be "No Heroics," meaning that if the patient refuses to eat, he is not to be fed by stomach tube; if he ceases to breathe, he is not to be put on a respirator. The doctor may also write on the chart, "D/C all meds," meaning to discontinue all medications. (As an aside, let me add that nurses not infrequently reported quietly to me— trusting me as a woman—that after such a D/C order, the patient seemed to improve and gain strength!)

If the patient was an abnormal new-born baby, whether it was abnormal externally or internally, we medical students were told to write on its chart, "Routine Care Only," and then let Nature deal as she saw fit with this mistake of her builders. This did not mean that the baby was not to be kept comfortable and pain-free, fed at the routine times, picked up and cuddled by the nurses. It meant that the child was to be spared the operations and injections that might be necessary to give it a workable body and be permitted to fade away.

Contacted in a Releasement session through the woman it was obsessing, a baby who had died after such an operation cried out in fear as it relived the opening procedures of the cardiac operation: "They are cutting me! They are cutting me!" (putting its thoughts into the woman's mind)

"Let your mind come here and be safe with us, and just see without pain or fear what they are doing to your body."

The child described the operation, though still sobbing softly at times.

"Honey," I told it, "you understand, don't you, that they are cutting you in order to help your little body be strong for you to live in. They are doing it to help you."

The baby seemed to understand but was still miserable. It admitted that its body, as born, could not have lived.

"What would you have preferred that they do, honey?" I asked. "What do you wish they had done instead?"

"Just love me, just hold me and love me," it said.

The parents thought they were showing a still greater love by having the doctors "cut" the baby, and the doctors sincerely thought they were helping it. Although I did not persist in questioning the reasons for such a brief lifetime, I felt that this baby had been destined to live only a matter of hours or minutes after birth, and it wanted only to be held and loved a while.

A word here might be appropriate about natural abortions. Nature does make mistakes, and when she is aware of such a mistake in an embryo she often begins trying to dispose of it. This usually occurs in the first trimester of pregnancy. If an abortion is threatening by bleeding or cramps, perhaps it is not wise to use "heroic" means too long to stop the bleeding, cause the cramps to cease, and prevent the spontaneous abortion, because when the child is born it may be found to be abnormal in some major way.

I am thinking just now of the baby born to a doctor and his wife when I was an intern. Two or three times there had been a threatened abortion, but the child was finally born at term, with severe hydrocephalus. The mother was not even allowed to see the baby with its huge head. It lived, lying in its crib, for at least a year, and the father told me that its head had become the same size around as his middle-aged waist. Nature had tried several times to dispose of the defective body but had been prevented by the medical personnel of the hospital, all with the very best of intentions. A Catholic nun said of one hydrocephalic child that "the eyes were pools of pain." Since increased intracranial pressure causes headaches, no doubt the nun's intuitive perception was accurate.

Induced Abortions

Abortions that are not spontaneous and natural really have no place in a chapter on Nature's Mercy, even though they may have been caused from merciful motives such as saving the mother's life or saving the unwanted child from a life of rejection, abuse, or post-natal murder in a parent's fit of rage. There is much emotion on both sides of the abortion question. Both sides have some truth to point out; both sides have some blind places in their vision.

When I was halfway through medical school I worked in a poverty-stricken hospital for women in the poor Irish Quarter of New Orleans. One of my first patients, whose medical history I was taking, listed her religion as Catholic. She was a heavy woman, in the hospital to have her eighth or ninth baby. I asked the routine question, "Have you ever had an abortion or miscarriage?"

"Oh yes," she said, matter-of-factly.

Her tone took me by surprise. "You mean you have had more than one?"

"Oh yes," in the same off-hand tone.

"You mean three? or four?"

"Oh, at least that many. The last time they almost killed me." She laughed. "They used slippery elm and it got me to bleeding and they couldn't get the bleeding stopped."

I looked at her chart. "But doesn't your religion forbid . . ."

She gave me a hard straight look. "Look, honey, you don't know that man of mine. I'd rather go ten times to a priest to confess an abortion than go two hundred times to confess using something. We just can't afford another mouth to feed. We can't take proper care of ones we have." She was no longer laughing.

I had thought her laughter meant she was hard and cold. Now I realized she had laughed because she was ashamed and embarrassed to have to tell her family secrets to a stranger.

A man friend once told me thoughtfully, "The Pope doesn't realize it, but he is encouraging abortions." Yes, as the woman said, she would rather confess ten abortions to a priest than two hundred times she had used contraceptives. A Catholic woman in Italy was quoted by an American reporter as saying of the Pope a few decades ago, "He no playa da game, he no maka da rules." This comment, aired on a television station, was of course never repeated; it offended too many people.

How can one avoid offending someone when discussing abortion? The "Pro-Choice" advocates are correct when they insist that the illegal abortions performed in back alleys and basements were often as crude and dangerous as the one described by my middle-aged Irish patient. Legalizing abortions reduced the number of maternal deaths—but greatly increased the number of fetal deaths.

The "Pro-Life" people are right when they insist that an embryo or fetus is alive, human, and sentient. They seem to forget, however, that after birth the person is still alive, human, and sentient, and being an unwanted child it can and often does suffer just as much as a fetus that is aborted. I wrote to one of the ministers of the Pro-Life movement some years ago, describing a picture I had seen in a medical journal: a ten-month-old baby boy, whose x-ray had revealed thirty old and new fractures of the tiny bones. The child was not crying—crying hurt the little broken ribs too much—but its face was a picture of pain and fear. The minister replied, admitting that he had not been aware of such aspects of the "Pro-life" movement, and said that now he didn't know what to think.

Meanwhile the movement goes on, and the common emotions of rage and hate are in themselves harmful to the unborn as well as to the mothers of the unborn. These emotional attitudes of the Pro-life people harm their own cause. Persons sympathetic with the unborn are repelled from the Pro-life movement by these excesses of rage and anger.

Three important attitudes toward sex need mention: First, that many persons have turned sex into a toy, a delightful plaything, a means of carefree pleasure. If there is any thought of possible pregnancy, it is with distaste, as toward an unpleasant possibility. If our pleasure results in such unwanted "consequences," we decide, thoughtlessly or otherwise, to eliminate the "consequences" and abort the contents of the uterus as "just a piece of meat." Better is the attitude of a Catholic lady who said, "Sex is a language of love." When two persons love each other they'll want to love and care for any children that come. The lady did agree that contraceptives were advisable.

The second attitude is the superstition among men of various countries, including the southern U.S., that if a man with a disease such as AIDS or gonorrhea has intercourse with a virgin, his disease will be dispelled. This belief is one reason that sometimes a child of five or six is found to be pregnant. Sex clinics in Zimbabwe find that young girls have a very high percentage of AIDS infection whereas young boys do not—the girls being the target for older men who are trying to get rid of their disease. The girls are being "used" selfishly by the men.

The third attitude is the common feeling that sex is a game, in which a boy may boast of how many girls he has gotten into "the family way," or a man may boast like an adolescent of how many women he has had sexual relations with (he usually expresses it more crudely). The attitude of men in the Army and other armed services, in any country, is often, "When you feel the urge, go get yourself a woman." This results, as one Army nurse remarked, that the men go "scattering babies all around the country" where they are stationed. The babies do not remain babies. They grow, they are considered "children of dust" by the people of the locale, abandoned by the fathers, unwanted by the mothers, ignored by the country of both father and mother. Yet biologically these "hybrid" children possess amazing and wonderful potentialities, as many hybrids do.

In our meditation group we were asked by one of the Masters to call the souls of infants and fetuses that had been aborted, killed by abuse, or exposed to die, and assist them to the Light. "So many little ones are suffering," he said. And in meditation Cynthia said she saw hundreds, thousands, of tiny bundles come floating at our call, "Most of them with girl children," she added. "So many of them! And even if we get all of them now, there will be more tomorrow." (You readers can also help as you meditate.)

I wish to quote a couple of paragraphs from the pages that I contributed to Dr. Winafred Lucas' manual on Regression Therapy (see Bibliography):

Expulsion of an entity by induced abortion of (its) fetal body, unless an understanding has previously been reached (between the soul of the fetus and the mother) can lead to karmic and emotional repercussions. One outcome is that the psyche of the fetus may flee the abortion scene and wander, frightened, in the earth-bound state for an indefinite period. Or it may seek warmth and refuge in some hiding place, such as the body of a living person, especially its mother, obsessing that person and bringing into that person all the fear, loneliness, and feelings of rejection and abandonment, the pain and anger, that the entity felt before and during the abortion procedure. Releasement not only frees the client from the obsessing infant-entity but also frees the frightened astral consciousness of the aborted infant from its fear and pains and assists it to go to the warmth and safety of a higher astral condition (sometimes called *The Summerland*), a garden-like state for children whose bodies have died. . . .

A woman who has had an abortion can talk to the infant's psyche, explaining why she felt it was wise to end the pregnancy and assuring the entity of the child that it was not a personal rejection of this particular soul but just a reluctance to have *any* child at this time. She may wish to add that at some later time she would welcome the entity as her child. This may be all that is necessary to alleviate the loneliness and sadness of the aborted psyche, whether or not it has been obsessing the mother in the literal sense.

Not only the consciousness of the aborted infant but also the mind of the mother can be eased by the simple means of just talking to the fetus, preferably aloud, when the woman is alone. The woman needs to be assured that she has not killed the soul of the child, only its body. And the child needs to be assured that the rejection was not a rejection of its personal self.

Several of us hypnotherapists have discovered that talking to a fetus *before* an abortion, explaining to it that its coming is unwelcome and that a delay would be better, has resulted in a natural, spontaneous abortion within a few days or weeks. (Several reports in Lucas' manual.) Such a result is not routine but occurs with fair frequency and is worth trying in any case, explaining to the soul of the fetus beforehand.

Let the Children Know

A final thought for those who have a child in a hospice: Children want to know about death and funerals, and they want to know what happens when people die. They see their friends in the hospice becoming more and more frail and weak and know that finally they die. They also see that dying can be peaceful. Near the end they begin to feel a quiet fearlessness, especially if a parent or nurse speaks to them of angel guardians, of heaven, or of Grandma or Grandpa waiting.

When my four sons were in junior high and high school we took a cable-car ride down into the Royal Gorge one day. As we slowly descended the steep canyon wall, one of my sons asked what would happen if the cable should break. I replied that there were two cables for safety, so if one broke the other was there to control the car.

"But what if both broke?" he wanted to know.

I looked far down the track to the distant bottom of the canyon. A huge rock was there, the river beyond it and at both sides. I could not see any possible chance of surviving physically if the cable-car went out of control and rushed down. And I had determined never to lie to my sons. Thinking fast I said, "Well, I suppose the next thing is that we'd be saying, 'My, Grandma, what a pretty dress you have on!'"

My mother, the boys' grandmother, had died two years before any of them were born. Their other grandmother was also dead. Now they digested my remark in silence.

(I had forgotten this little incident long ago, but one of my sons reminded me of it. *He* had not forgotten!)

IO

WE SURVIVORS

DURING THE TERMINAL PERIOD the relatives and friends of the person dying tend to fall into two groups: those that are able to let go, and those who deny that death is approaching their loved one and fight against its approach. There is also a middle group, those who know that death is coming but who are not able to keep themselves from stalling it off as long as possible, even when their rational minds know that the body of their loved invalid has no future usefulness.

In this third group my sister and I found ourselves when our father became helpless. Almost apologetically she told me that when he developed a fever in the nursing home and his doctor asked whether she wanted him to be given injections of an antibiotic, she could not refuse her dad this help. She and I both knew that our dad's old body could never be adequate for him to live in—and yet she could not bring herself to let him continue to burn with fever. I understood her feelings. In fact, after he was moved to a place nearer to me and began running another fever, I, as his doctor, after an inward argument with my own common sense mind, gave him an injection of antibiotic, brought the fever down, and made him more comfortable—for a few weeks more of helplessness. It was only when he began to spike a third fever that I finally was able to let go—allowing Nature to have her way with him.

174

If my sister and I were to live over again those months, we might very well make different decisions. We knew that our dad wanted to go to be with our mother, who had died ten years before. It was not for his sake that we kept his body alive; it was for our own sakes, and because we just could not, at that time, make a different decision. No rational explanation.

Another example of not letting the patient go is the work of Lanetta, my retired Army nurse friend. She went to a distant state to visit her aged aunt, who was quite ill, and Lanetta found herself becoming a full-time nurse to Aunt M. Lanetta could tell that it was only a matter of time before Aunt M. would pass on. But week after week went by, then month after month, and still Aunt M. hung on. Lanetta could not understand how, in Aunt M.'s condition, she could still live. I reminded her, "Well, you know that she has excellent nursing care . . . and that means when her blood pressure goes up, she is given something to bring it down. When her appetite falls off, she is urged to eat and tempted with flavorsome foods. If she gets an infection, it is treated and the germs are killed." Even after my pointing out these things to her, Lanetta did not see why her aunt was still holding onto life. But could she have resisted the strong inclination to fulfill these deeply ingrained nursing techniques, even to let Aunt M. pass on peacefully?

Sometimes it is the emotional dependency of one or more survivors on a metaphysical level that hold a dying person back from freedom. I was present at an evening family gathering of friends a good many years ago and some tape recordings of the mother's own little songs and other compositions was played. Smiling, I turned to her and complemented her on her songs. Tears came into her eyes.

"I can't remember writing them. I just can't remember anything like that. . . . Why can't I go?" And the little woman broke down and wept. Later when my friend and I talked about her mother, she said it was not she herself but a sister who was holding the mother, unable to let go emotionally. The sister was even accusing my friend of not taking adequate care of the mother. Unfortunately, the sister lived at a distance so that she was not aware of just how well the mother was being cared for. My friend, too, was holding the mother's body here.

Prayers for the terminal person have been known to accomplish miraculous recoveries that have amazed doctors and friends. One woman, telling her story to the magazine *Guideposts* some years ago, said that she and her daughters prayed earnestly and with tears for the life of their husband and father, who had been severely brain-injured in an accident. Their prayers were answered: the man did live, but as a vegetable, unable to feed himself or speak. The mother urged the readers of her story, "Be careful what you pray for, and pray for whatever is best—pray for God's will, not for your own will."

A story that was unfolding for almost six years is that of a dear lady in western Colorado who was diagnosed at the age of eighty-two as having breast cancer. She accepted the usual treatments but eventually was told that the growth had metastasized and that no more surgery could be done. Philosophically she prepared to die and allowed a young woman news reporter for the *Grand Junction Daily Sentinel* to follow the course of her remaining months under the caption of "Dying with Dignity." She kept expecting, each night, to fall asleep and die, and each morning was disappointed to find herself still in her body. Even so, she remained cheerful for several years, witty and quick to see the comical side of things. Then she began to find it more difficult to keep her sense of humor and her *joie de vivre*, as she called it, the "joy of living."

Although she was not Catholic, she visited the Trappist monastery at Snowmass and with tears admitted her discouragement to gentle white-bearded Father Theophane there, wondering why she could not die. Father Theophane told her, *"As long as you are living, live!"* And for much of the time after that she did a remarkably good job of following his wise advice.

Almost six years went by after the first diagnosis of cancer. At each examination, although the cancer was mentioned routinely, the report usually concluded with, "Findings consistent with age of patient." She was having a hard time keeping her usual cheerful disposition. (Such a change in personality is often associated with aging.) But the headline of one late installment of her story (Sept. 17, '95) was, "I'm perked up. I *do* have cancer." She added, "I'd be terrified if I didn't. If Hospice had discarded me, I'd be in an awful way."

"Her strange longevity has jeopardized hospice care," said the reporter.

Several friends of mine were following her story. They told me that at first they prayed that she might recover; later that she might continue to live and feel well; more recently that she might die, as she wished. I wonder what sort of fabric we would see if that interwoven web of everyone's prayers for her were visible! The total effect seems to have been continued life for nearly six years, much of the time pain-ridden, it is true, but a worthwhile life in many ways. She was able to see the theater production of one of the plays she had written long ago and to receive plaudits as the author from her wheelchair. Finally she was able to let go even the *joie de vivre* and permit herself to go on.

She was the patient, but wasn't she also a survivor, even if against her own will? How can one evaluate the influence her story has had on all the readers of it? Her courage and staunch trust in the overall plan of the universe shone through to all who read it, just as the pathos and the times of discouragement and tears called forth sympathy and tenderness toward her and all who face similar situations.

Care-givers Are Human, Too

During the weeks or months of a person's long illness the care-givers need all the patience and sturdiness of character that they have in order to remain cheery and unfatigued. In fact, these qualities may be almost impossible to maintain day after day, week after week, especially if the patient becomes irritable and demanding.

There is a natural tendency for care-givers to give in to the demands of the one who is sick or ailing, especially if the patient is very young, very old, or very petulant. Too much overly-soft attention results in a patient who becomes "spoiled" and self-centered, insensitive to the needs and natural limitations of the care-givers. Too little TLC ("tender loving care"), however, results in the patient's feeling of being a burden, of being resented, and the patient's feeling of being rejected may cause periods of tearfulness or a dropping into depression.

It is difficult to walk a firm wise pathway between spoiling the patient and allowing her or him to feel neglected and burdensome. The care-givers do get tired. And the patient's brain-cells do become clogged with toxins or with the tangles of Alzheimer's disease, or just become old and ready to die. When the physical brain cells suffer these deteriorations, the disposition of the patient reveals the changes in negative ways. It may help the care-givers to understand that the bursts of irritability, the resentful remarks, the frettings and accusations of the patient are not representative of the true nature of the person but are only a reflection of the limitations of the physical brain. Let the care-givers continue to be as patient as possible, and not allow these problems to be taken personally.

Over a period of months or years, the care-givers may become so over-worked and fatigued that resentment increases in spite of themselves. They are having to give up their own time, their own life, to the invalid. They may even have secret thoughts of what a relief the death of the invalid would be.

All this is understandable; it is almost natural, even if not desirable. Let the tired, worn care-givers simply look honestly at these feelings, acknowledge their presence, and arrange to rest each day, take a real vacation if possible, pray for strength and patience and gentleness, and take up the task again, with a helper if possible. If the invalid is conscious and has insight as to her own incompetence, her feelings of humiliation and unworthiness cause her as much anguish as the secret resentment and fatigue cause her care-giver. And she may be longing for death far more acutely than the care-giver's secret thought.

After the Death of the Invalid

When at last the patient ceases to breathe, the care-giver, especially if a relative, may experience a surge of mixed emotions. There may be genuine grief combined with enormous relief and probably some guilty feelings along with the latter.

Guilt. One of the strongest and most long-lasting of the negative emotions, and one that occurs again and again in the survivors: "If only I had ___"; "I promised him, but I never got around to ___"; "Now it's too late ___"

Dear care-givers, you are worn out with much physical and emotional stress. It is time for you to rest first, and evaluate the situation later when your mind is clear and your body revitalized and nourished. And then, remember, your former invalid is probably still near, but in any event is still in mental contact with you. Just *accept her understanding and forgiveness* and say, "I love you and I am glad you are free and well!" And then put away the guilt and take up life again.

Emotions of Survivors After the Death

Your life will need adjustment with new things to fill the many hours that are now empty of the former duties. One of the very first duties will be to inform friends of the death. You may find yourself writing, or saying on the phone, "She passed away." "She departed." "She left us."

These phrases seem to imply more or less active movement on the part of the one deceased, even an acceptance of departure by the dying person. Might this feeling on the part of some survivors be a reason for the anger that is sometimes found underlying the grief?

I remember the first time such anger was called to my attention. I had mentioned the grief of my father after my mother's sudden death following a simple operation. The doctor to whom I was speaking added, "—and anger."

Surprised, I asked, "Why should my father be angry? She couldn't help dying!"

"'Darn you—you went away and left me!'" the doctor said.

"Oh . . . I see . . . but my father would not have *felt* it as anger," was my reply. My father was not the angry type. But his grief was profound and long-lasting. When I tried to remind him that he knew she was not dead, he said, his voice quivering, "All I know is that she isn't here."

How we depend on our physical senses for our beliefs! And our entire culture, for the past century or more, has been to sweep away as worthless any "beliefs" that cannot be tested and measured by physical means.

I have wished many times that I had realized that there are different ways in which people respond to a death; I could have been far more supportive to my dad in his loneliness if I had understood that after the shock of a sudden death there is a natural wrenching of the entire being of the closest survivors. A sympathetic silence would have been much more tender. (My guilt!)

"I promised her," said that my father, "that when I retired I would take her to the Hawaiian Islands—and I never did." (His guilt!)

The reason he could not take her traveling was because I had to retire from my work for reasons of health and needed a place to live while my husband was in the Service; so I was basically the reason why my father could not fulfill his promise. (More guilt? Well, at least deep regret and sorrow.)

After perceiving these feelings, then talk to the deceased one, expressing to him or her what you feel and why, and then *accept the forgiveness and take up your life again* with a deep breath of release and new resolution. As I have said before, *after* death a person understands and can change much more easily than before death. The continuing grief and guilt of the survivors only cause continued sorrow for the deceased loved ones.

Patterns of Survivors' Reaction to Death

Whether or not a survivor consciously feels loss, grief, or anger, those emotions may have a self-centered element. The survivor may be grieving for himself, for the change in his life, for the loss of someone who had furnished comfort and security, pleasure or companionship. All of these seem to have been taken away by the death of the loved one, leaving the survivor the poorer and therefore distraught and even angry. Children too young to understand death may feel a sense of betrayal, of desertion, and feel rejected or angry at the abandonment. The *conscious* anger of an older person may be turned toward Fate or God.

If the survivors are emotionally of a different type or have a firm belief in an afterlife, there may be less of the inward turned grief and more thought about the deceased person's own feelings: "She had a hard life. Now she can be at peace." "It was a tough haul for him. I'm glad he doesn't have to suffer any more."

To some people of still another type, statements like these may seem to indicate less love for the deceased. Such persons may feel that a burst of audible grief and repeated statements about their "loss" show their deeper love. This attitude may be cultural, the expected reaction of survivors during an expected "mourning period": "I'll weep my weep, wail my wail."

Outward expressions of grief, however, are not a good indication of the actual feelings in many people. The opposite extreme is the complete suppression of any show of emotion after a death. This outwardly maintained emotional calm, whether based on a religion or not, may be due to a denial of the fact of death or it may indicate a deep conviction that any show of grief is weak, childish—an infantile crybaby propensity. Such persons may feel superior to those who openly express grief.

If deep emotions are suppressed, kept internal, this is not emotionally healthy. It may result in a true *repression* of feelings of grief so that there is no longer any conscious recognition of such feelings at all, not even numbness—not until some later event opens up the subconscious memory and allows the repressed emotions to surface uncontrollably, with unexpected suddenness. This is a frequent pattern for repressed feelings.

There are some people who exhibit a genuine calm after a death. It may resemble repression but is very different: a peaceful, quiet, even though perhaps sad acceptance of the death. It may be that they have already done their grieving before the death. Or their accepting attitude may be based upon a religious conviction of continued livingness after bodily death, or else paradoxically upon a calm, strong, though probably sorrowful conviction of the total extinction of the life of the dead.

These latter persons, undeniably brave and courageous, may be aware of their courage and feel somewhat superior to those who "believe in an afterlife because they can't face the fact of dying," or words to that effect, implying that all who "believe in" an afterlife are not as brave as they are. Well, that may be true in some or even many instances, but not all. And those who "believe in" an afterlife may look with secret (or open) scorn at those who "believe in" total annihilation of consciousness at death. (A whole volume could be written about "Scorn in Secret Places!" Or should it be entitled, "Self-righteousness All Over"?)

I want to remind all of us that birth occurs without the prerequisite of any Belief in Birth. So does death occur without any Belief in Dying. And so does continued consciousness after death occur without any particular Belief. Did you hear me, friends?

Let me digress for a moment to tell you how I became and then unbecame an atheist. In high school I began to ask why a merciful Creator created warped deformed bodies or retarded minds that almost compelled the suffering of the entity that would live in such a handicapped body or limited brain-capacity. Was that justice?

I could think of a thousand other things that denied the mercy and justice of the world. I decided I would get even with such an irrational Creator by disbelieving in Him. So I did! Childish, you say? Yes, I admit it, but I was angry at the injustices I saw all around me, while I myself and my girlhood family were mostly protected.

My father, however, had instilled in us children a profound respect and admiration for the marvelous forms of Nature in all her infinite variations. In high school English class I suddenly realized that I could write a better story than the Creator had, if the Creator indeed made these wonderful creations and creatures and then just tossed them into the garbage as trash after a minute speck of Time in His limitless Infinity. Phooey on that, I said. Blasphemy, you say? Probably. But I was defiant and felt myself waving my tiny ant-antennae in the face of the Infinite Universe and any God who might be up there . . . and being unafraid. "If you really are God, you understand!"

If such a God were to be angry and squash this little ant, how would that be much different from His letting the ant live another few infinitesimal split specks of Infinity and THEN get squashed?

Well, the ant didn't get squashed. Instead, I began to realize that the idea of any living creature's being created only to be totally annihilated was totally irrational. In fact, I saw the plan of the Universe become ever more wide, broad, deep, and high the longer I contemplated any aspect of it, whether in the visible physical realm or in the invisible psychological and spiritual realms. The Creator to me is no longer the elderly, bearded, white, male, *human*, being depicted so graphically by Michelangelo and others but is a vast Intelligence, Compassion, Power, and Plan which encompasses not only human beings, not only this planet, not only this galaxy, but truly the Universe, and maybe lots more universes in still undiscovered frequencies. Do we really know it all yet? And this all-pervading Power and

Compassion is also all-embracing Love and Understanding, not to be feared but trusted as a tender parent. It understands, whether we call it Father, or God, or Allah, or Yahweh.

We don't know it all in the psychospiritual realms, either. The injustices that I see throughout the world are judged to be injustices from the superficial view. When we inquire more deeply into the causes of each individual example, we begin to find reasons which, especially after examining the previous lives of a sufferer, explain much, as detailed at length in previous chapters.

Signals of Approaching "Right Time"

The following signals are ones that I have observed down the years in various cases, but are not to be considered a list of definite and infallible signs of approaching death at all.

During the several weeks and months before my mother suddenly died (four days after removal of a benign ovarian tumor), she had a number of delightful little experiences and had received some unexpected little gifts: letters, souvenirs. She was happy and felt well. A friend from her college days, a Japanese man, had dropped by for a visit. She and my father had not seen him for many years and it was a delight for both to see him again. There were similar pleasant surprises.

After her death I began to feel that maybe, on some unconscious level, a part of her knew that her time was near and was hastening to fulfill as many last pleasures as possible, to tie up as many loose ends as the time permitted, so that her life was rounded up.

Only two weeks later my "other mother" died, Mrs. Ward, the lovely New England widow with whom I had stayed during my two years in Massachusetts while working at Mt. Holyoke College. It was a sobering event, to "lose" two such dear close people within so short a time.

Mrs. Ward's son told me that during the months before her death she had been able to take several short trips to places she had wanted to see, had received visitors whom she had not seen for years, had received little gifts from me and from others, and in general had really enjoyed those months. Again it felt to me as if a life was being rounded up in preparation for its ending.

Since then (1946) I have kept an open eye for similar events in the lives of relatives and friends. One that especially seemed noticeable was in the summer of 1991 when I was spending a few days with Agnes, a college friend and former room-mate, in the mountain cabin that she and her husband used as a summer home. With electricity but no telephone nor television, she had plenty of time for reading and writing. She showed me a long list of names.

"I've written or sent little tokens to all of these people," she told me proudly. "I'm really getting caught up on my correspondence."

In that instant my mind sprang to the alert. During the days following I watched, but perceived no hint that Agnes suspected what I was suspecting. She was her same cheery, intelligent, witty self. Nor did her husband Ernest seem different in any way. I was the only one with silent wonderings.

The next January Agnes had a stroke. Then a second one, and a third, and a fourth as the months rolled by. She was now hemiplegic. A blood clot obstructing the blood flow in one leg necessitated amputation. She was bedfast. That is when at last I wrote Ernest what I had wondered about the previous summer. "I think some unconscious part of her knew that her time was coming and she was tying up loose ends and filling up little gaps in her contacts with friends while she could."

Even then, with her speech impaired, Agnes seemed to be mentally alert. She could converse with me when I drove to Ogden, Utah, to visit her after her sixth stroke. One day, looking up from her bed, she asked piteously, "Louise, Louise, Louise—Why? Why? Why?"

"Agnes, I don't know why. We don't know why your sister had her stroke, either. But sometime I believe we will know why."

She focused intensely on my eyes and I saw understanding come into hers when I mentioned her sister's stroke. The sister had lived for quite a number of years after a severe stroke. I saw that until now Agnes had not equated her own condition with that of Lucille's wheelchair existence.

Agnes and Ernest had no interest in my hypnotic work and I respected their choices and opinions. Once, however, when Agnes fell asleep while I was reading to her, I did take the opportunity to speak to her as she slept (sleep learning).

Later I told Ernest about it. "I told her that soon she might come to a fork in the path, and either she or God would choose which path to take—but either way, it would be all right."

Tears came to his eyes, and yet I felt that somehow my words had released him from any feelings that he must do everything and anything to keep her body alive. He told me the next day that he had decided, "No more surgery"— because a clot was forming in the other leg and a second amputation had been discussed. This second clot was a clear signal to him, so that he was able to let her go—to let her body go.

A few weeks later she died very quietly on Thanksgiving Day. Ernest wound up the rest of his business affairs, sold his house, and within a few years he, too, made the Transition.

The sequence of events in Agnes' story is another of the signals that may indicate approaching Transition: a series of signs that the body is wearing out —a series of heart attacks, a series of strokes, and so on. Yet do not take these as solid evidence of approaching death! Each individual case has to be considered individually. Just be aware that such a series might indicate that an ending is approaching for the body. Loss of appetite may be another signal, with loss of weight and energy. It does not hurt to recall now and then that, as elderly Reverend Charles Girelius wrote in one of his poems, "My body is a candle meant to be consumed."

Buddha taught that whatever has a beginning formed by the coming-together of different parts will also have an ending when those component elements fall apart and the thing that was a whole disintegrates. "How could it be otherwise?" he asked. Or to put it in more familiar terms, "Nothing is sure but death and taxes." (The "taxes" part is for someone else to write a book about.)

Survivors After a Sudden Death

Much of what has been said applies to the survivors after any type of death. The abruptness of a sudden death, however, causes a period of shock and confusion, and of either numbness or extreme emotions, of which grief is only one.

If the death occurred by an accident, the survivors have pain and grief but may also have a tendency to blame and be very angry at whatever or whoever is felt to have caused the accident. Anger and resentment usually follow a death from the mistake of a doctor or nurse or from an attack by another person. War deaths, suicides, and abortions account for many abrupt Transitions and leave the survivors with varying feelings and duties.

If the body of the deceased person is there to be taken care of (it may not be, after a death in battle or an abortion), then there is the funeral to be planned, announcements to be sent to newspapers, and all the legal procedures that occupy the time and thoughts of the survivors. This activity may not be entirely on the negative side. It serves as an interlude during which the thoughts of the survivors begin to become accustomed to the idea of no longer seeing or hearing their loved one.

It is after this interlude that the realization of the loved one's "loss" may be felt much more keenly. One survivor said, "The loneliness really hits after all the sympathy cards have been received and all the relatives have gone home and the neighbors don't come around any more."

Talismans and Souvenirs

People differ. Some react to death in one way, others in an entirely opposite way. Some, for instance, hoard all the earthly possessions of the deceased one; others want to get all such possessions out of sight, given away, sold, whatever.

A good many people do like to keep a few precious souvenirs of their "departed" loved one. To some people these may be nothing more than souvenirs, tangible memories; to others they may be talismans of far greater meaning and far closer contact.

A few examples will illustrate these differences.

When my parents were married in 1911, my father gave as a wedding ring a family heirloom ring of 18 karat gold, a heavy gold band. After my mother died, the mortuary handed him an envelope in which was a lock of her hair—and the wedding band. He was shaken. "It was hers. I wanted it to be buried with her. She had never taken it off."

To my father the ring was a symbol of the truest union down through the generations in his family. "She had never taken it off"—and now a stranger had taken it from her finger, a desecration of her defenseless lifeless body.

From my own personal feelings I told him earnestly, "It's all right. It was yours to begin with, now it is yours again. You wear it now. It will fit your little finger, won't it?"

With some hesitation, which I did not understand, he did just this, and after a while I believe he felt that it was right. It was now a talisman of her nearness, still her ring, as if she had given it back to him to wear.

For all the rest of her belongings, however, his attitude seemed totally strange to me. He seemed to want to get everything that was a reminder of her completely out of his sight—or perhaps that was merely my interpretation. My mother's two sisters and we two daughters were there for the funeral, plus one of my father's sisters and a dear sister-in-law. He informed us that he would take these two for a long ride while the four of us blood relatives went through all of my mother's belongings and divided them among us: clothing, jewelry, keepsakes, everything.

Thus it was that the four of us gathered in the bedroom and I reached first of all for the wooden box in which she kept her jewelry—a few "good" pieces, most just little tokens given to her by friends or relatives. Ruby's eyes lit up at the sight of the old cigar box with a girl's face on it in profile, her long flowing hair streaming back.

"My burnt-wood box that I made for Myrtle's wedding," she cried. Fifteen years younger than her sister, she was barely thirteen when she made that attractive box. We insisted that she take it back now, but for the moment we just passed it around the circle, each of us taking back the trinkets we had given to mother or sister:

"Oh, this string of spool-knitted beads—I remember when I made this for her." "And this little artificial-ivory rosebud—I sent her that from college!" " Look, here are the gold earrings I gave her," and so on.

By and by Ruby said, "I don't want you to misunderstand me—but isn't this fun?"

Yes, it truly was fun. It had turned out to be the most intimate and joyous sort of memorial service anyone could have imagined, just this spontaneous sharing of memories and reminders of the happiness we four had given, memories carefully saved in the precious old burnt-wood box. Now we were getting back that happiness.

"It is just as if she is here enjoying the fun with us," I agreed, not knowing then what I know now but feeling the truth of what I said.

Later, after the rest had all returned to their homes and I was going through some last articles of clothing, I came upon a comfortable old girdle that she had mended, patched, and re-patched very neatly. It was spotlessly clean but definitely old and worn—it was just like her to keep such a thing. I decided to keep it for a souvenir—until I heard her say, almost audibly, "Ah, honey, you don't want that old thing!"

I realized that it would embarrass her if I kept it, so I didn't. It will embarrass her for me to tell about it now, but I'm reminding her that the story may help someone who may read it: Don't keep old things that have no use or beauty—unless they do have real inner beauty of memory for you and won't make your loved one *too* embarrassed on the other side!

A lock of the deceased one's hair seems to be saved routinely by the mortuary and given to each of the survivors. This, too, "has the vibrations on it," as the young folk say.

This little story is about two small girls whose mother had had a nervous breakdown and placed the children in an orphanage, never to return for them or contact them. The two little sisters were inseparable, clinging to each other. Then one of them died, and the nuns running the orphanage took charge of her body, pushing away the other sister to do so. One of the older girls at the orphanage, however, sneaked a lock of the dead girl's hair to the surviving sister. That lock of hair was the most precious possession that Mary had, a tiny bit of her beloved sibling.

At Easter someone gave each child at the orphanage one colored Easter egg. Mary cherished her beautiful bright egg; it was the second most precious thing she owned. These two things were hers. But when she was old enough to be lent out to a farm family as a hired girl working for room and board, her few small belongings were packed for her, and the lock of hair and the Easter egg (long since cracked and dried up inside) were discovered and confiscated. Mary was in her eighties when she told me this story; she could chuckle, but I knew the laughter covered a memory of deep loss and emptiness. The lock of hair in particular was her touchable contact with her dead sister. From then on she had to find companionship in the invisible ways of prayer and religion.

If a survivor is like Mary, a little talisman of the loved one who has died is a true warm channel of communication and love. A second little story illustrates what a wide variation there may be in such talismans:

When I was a medical student, we sometimes made house calls as part of our training. On one such "field trip" our small section (about sixteen male students and I, the one female) visited a boarder in the home of a middle-aged widow in one of the poorer parts of New Orleans. I noticed the landlady beckoning me to come away from the group of students. She led me, as if on a secret mission, toward the old upright piano, reached up behind a picture, and brought down a small jar to show me.

"My husband's finger," she whispered. "He got it infected so bad the doctor had to take it off. I kept it. It's a comfort to me since he's gone."

To tell the truth, I thought it was a rather gruesome sort of souvenir, if she were looking for souvenirs. A pickled finger? Better to have the doctor drop it in the garbage to be incinerated, no? No. Not when it meant so much of warmth and love to her.

I was reminded of that finger when I saw in the August, 1995, *National Geographic Magazine* a picture of a weeping Japanese woman with a pure white, delicately decorated package on her lap, the ashes of her father who had been killed in the explosion over Hiroshima fifty years ago. The ashes had never been claimed until now because of a misspelling of the name on the package. The picture echoed the woman's word, "Let's go home now, Father." That daughter will feel freer and less lonely now. Souvenirs and talismans do have a profound value to many persons.

There are souvenirs of less material form, such as a song, a poem, a certain day of the year, which a survivor may hold in a special place in his heart in memory of the deceased one. Any and all of these are fine except when they become fetishes to cling to and prevent the surviving one from gathering his courage and getting on with his life. The location of a grave may seem to be more sacred than other places and the loved one may seem nearer there, but this is an illusion, even though a comforting illusion. There is no harm unless pilgrimages to the grave become a compulsion or a fixation, usurping the life of the survivor. Then the survivor needs the warm human contact of a support group or professional help, especially spiritual or religious in orientation, or even the companionship of a puppy or kitten with its playful, innocent, distracting reminders that life and affection go on.

Survivors Who Hear from Their Loved Ones

Although a few who watch by the bedside of a dying one have reported seeing a mist or vaporous cloudlike body rising from the dying physical body and floating above it or moving to another location in the room, most of us do not have this type of psychic sensitivity well enough developed. For most of us there is no reception of the efforts of the deceased to comfort us, probably because of our concentration on the vacated physical body.

Telepathic communication between the deceased one and the survivor appears to occur with relative frequency between husband and wife and between child and grandparent, in my practice. I have read of studies which report that about fifty percent of widows and widowers feel that they have received communications from the deceased spouse in some manner: visually, audibly, or in clear telepathic thought reception.

This is so convincing and common a phenomenon that I do not hesitate to write to widowed friends about it, asking that they remain open to the possibility of "hearing" from their recently deceased loved one sometime in a quiet moment. The responses in letters to me have corroborated my confidence.

Sometimes the contact from the deceased one comes as a symbol. A close friend whose husband had died wrote me that she appreciated my letter asking her to be open to receive any message from Charlie that might come. "You are the only person I can talk to, about things like this, " she said, "and you are the only one who will understand when 1 say that I did get a message from Charlie. Just as I was sitting quietly at a window watching the sunset colors fading, a great shooting star traveled across the sky and I saw Charlie's hand throwing it to me and heard his voice saying, 'Don't be so *serious! I'm all right!*'"

My rational mind could not help wondering if this interpretation of a meteor might be the result of her desire for such a meaning. Knowing something of the powers of the subconscious and superconscious minds, however, and of the miraculous ways in which we are interconnected with one another and with the universe, and seeing how helpful this experience had been to a lonely friend, I accepted it as she related it, along with her interpretation. Who am I to judge? I might make a compromise interpretation to myself that Charlie knew the meteor was going to stream across the twilight sky and he took advantage of the quietness, the beauty of the evening, and the streak of light to contact his wife's mind and enable her to see his hand and hear his voice. (The comical part to me is that both of these dear people claimed to be atheists. I didn't believe that claim literally, either!)

An unknown number of psychically sensitive persons have had *spontaneous visions* or audible contacts with their loved ones. Several of my friends are sensitives of this type. After Lanetta's husband Jerry died, it was our mutual friend, Virginia, who first saw Jerry in Lanetta's house, sitting there smiling at all of us. After this Lanetta also could see him at times. For a while Jerry took a mischievous pleasure in tinkering with the electric clocks and the cuckoo clock, until Lanetta in exasperation told him that she already knew he was there and he could stop the nonsense. Only much later, when he was still in the earth plane though at ease and free, did she advise him to go on to the higher plane.

"I'm all right and can take care of myself," she assured him.

Since then she has not seen him, but we know that we could call him back if there was reason to do so.

A third woman friend, Albie of Czechoslovakian birth, is a sensitive, too. After graduate school she married a Brazilian doctor and moved to Rio de Janeiro. When her Luys died she knew the exact time of his Transition in the hospital many blocks away. He came visibly to her bedroom door at home and for a moment just stood there looking at her before fading from her sight.

She went periodically to his tomb with flowers and would remain there for a while, thinking about him. Sometimes she would see him, sometimes not, but the contacts were warm until one certain day. That day he did appear to her, but his eyes were focused far away, looking toward the mountains. He had never spoken audibly to her but she often heard his thoughts. This day she could make out nothing but a deep sadness and a fleeting idea that it was his daughter who was in his mind. Later that same day, after she was back home again, she received word that her stepdaughter had been severely injured in an accident when the car she was in went over a steep grade in the mountains. The young woman lived but was brain-injured. Albie felt that her husband knew about the accident, perhaps just as it was occurring, and his sadness transmitted itself to her in the cemetery.

All these things she told me in long letters written in odd Czechoslovakian flavored English.

Calling Back the Loved One

In a hypnotic session with the survivor in hypnosis, the deceased soul will come in answer to an invitation from the facilitator and will be seen by the survivor either as a full (astral) body identifiable as the deceased, as just the face, or as an object symbolic of the entity. A widow, a friend of mine, saw only her dead husband's shoes when he came in response to our call. She said he had been proud of having immaculate shoes and would shine and polish them every week.

The husband of a nurse-friend had been an artist. He presented himself as a flood of beautiful color to Charlene while she was in hypnosis. She herself interpreted the color, following the thoughts that he gave her—thoughts entirely different from my own and even from hers! She saw "red"— which I feared meant something related to danger, like a warning, or else to anger or resentment. She wanted to get a message for "peace and tranquillity."

But she said, choking back tears, "It means *activity*— going back to work, I guess, and I *don't want* to go back to work! But he says, 'Activity.'"

I could not help agreeing with the husband that it would be best for Charlene to return to her nursing and feel the satisfaction of knowing she was helping others while at the same time distracting her mind from her loneliness. She did go back to work, and later was very glad that she had.

Another example of a symbol being sent by the deceased one occurred in a hypnotic session with a young married woman whose first love was killed in an accident when both were only teenagers. She still loved him and each year on the anniversary of his death she took roses to his grave. She said she would like to have a contact with him.

In answer to my invitation to "Please come, if you are willing and if it is permissible," the girl said, "I see roses." Slowly she added, "Red roses . . . but I always took pink roses to his grave."

Occasionally, as in this instance, I do ask a leading question in order to direct the client's mind to inquire as to the correct meaning of a symbol or dream.

"Do you think that he chose red roses on purpose? Maybe to tell you that he is truly alive, not in the grave to which you always brought pink roses?"

She deliberated a moment and then agreed. After the session was over she seemed satisfied and relaxed though rather pensive. Her smile was quiet but her eyes were clear, not sad.

One more example of a woman who contacted her loved one through hypnosis is the following, actually the first time I attempted this sort of contact. The young married woman asked if I could somehow help her find out what had caused the crash of the small plane in which her first husband and all the crew had died. The mechanics at the airport said the plane had been in perfect condition on takeoff.

"Everyone says it must have been pilot error," she said, "but I am a pilot myself, and I know that my husband was a good pilot. I want to know what went wrong, just for my own peace of mind."

I had never undertaken such a task before, but if no one else knew how to tackle the problem, I could try, trusting the knowledge and power of the subconscious and super-conscious aspects of the minds of all three of us, including her deceased husband.

With the young woman in hypnosis I asked her to let her mind fly alongside the plane and observe, without emotion, what happened. She saw a sudden gust of wind hit the plane and knock it off balance.

I asked her to go back to the same moment in time and this time be inside the plane, again without emotion, and hear and see what was going on. She felt the shock of the wind gust, saw a chair in the cabin of the plane come loose and begin banging around, heard the shouts of the four or five crew members, and her husband's shout, "I can't hold her! We're going down!"

At this point I had her send her mind outside the plane and just watch the following events as an observer, again without emotion (although some emotion did leak through, understandably). She saw the plane struggling for control, saw it nose-dive into the mountainside, and "everything just rolls up like a ball!" she exclaimed. Then she saw the burst of fire, which consumed plane and crew so completely that only the pilot's body could be identified afterward and then only because his wallet was found nearby.

Through careful wordings I had been able to prevent her from feeling too much of the anguish associated with seeing all this. One main source of her sorrow was, "I never got to tell him good-bye."

"Would you like to contact him now to tell him good-bye?" I asked, on impulse.

So, when she acquiesced, I said, "We are calling you, 'Jim.' Please come. Your wife would like to contact you."

He did come, appearing to her and conversing with her. But the next day she phoned and asked if we could have another session to meet with him again. "He didn't seem quite natural; he didn't seem warm, as if he really didn't want to talk to me."

"I know—I know what was wrong," I hurried to say. "I should have asked his permission first and given him a little time, a short notice of our intention, so he could adjust to the idea of returning to this lower vibration. And besides, you told me that he didn't believe in an after-life, while you did. He might have been wondering when you were going to say, 'I told you so.'"

The second session went very smoothly. Almost before I finished a polite invitation, asking his permission, his wife began to smile. "I see somebody," she said.

"Is it your husband?"

"Yes, he's smiling. He says, 'You were right.'"

She asked him some questions about her plans for a future occupational course. After she told him what she had suddenly thought of, "a *combination* of veterinary work and work with old people—Pet Therapy!"—he agreed, "Right on! That's it."

This time when she came back to normal awareness she was happy and satisfied, not only with the warm contact with her former husband but also with his confirmation of her sudden insight as to what her future course in life might be. There was no "good-bye" after all. She said he turned back and waved as he was leaving.

I might wonder if it was Jim who put into her mind the idea of combining her two deep interests as Pet Therapy. I did not think to ask him, nor did she, and he did not inform us. But it could have been. His intellect was clear and his perception of the future much clearer than ours. He was and is not simply a "shade" or a "ghost" but still a "people."

II

DEATH COMES
FOR ANIMALS, TOO

HOW MANY MILLIONS OF PET OWNERS have had times of grief over
the injury or death of a loved pet? Would it change anything
for a sorrowing pet owner if we knew how many millions of
others had a similar sorrow? Numbers do not offer solace,
nor the knowing all along that a pet will probably die before
the owner. These do not ease the pain of "losing" a beloved
companion.

Pet owners feel that the animal is more than a mere
animal. We often hear someone say, "This dog doesn't know
it isn't people" or "My cat (or parrot) is a real member of the
family." This feeling is one form of real love, the trust and
faithfulness of the animal and the affection of the human
owner.

There are less warm attitudes toward animals, too, attitudes of exploitation, of using the animals as insentient
objects for what good they can be to human beings. Then
there are the cults which still perform animal sacrifices in
their rituals and use animals as a means to obtain something
that they desire.

Whether or not the human being considers the animal to
have intelligence and feelings or a soul makes no difference:

all evidence obtained, not only by my own experiences through hypnotic contacts but by those of other therapists and psychics as well, indicates that animals do indeed possess a continuing consciousness that persists past the death of its physical form. This has been called the animal soul.

The Pool of Consciousness

The consciousness of animals while living and after death seems to belong to a Collective Consciousness/Unconscious for each species. This pool therefore receives all the individual experiences of the members of that species and gradually becomes pervaded throughout the whole by the sum of the life-experiences of the individuals. Animals that have had long-term or intense relationships with human beings, however, may have developed a set of human-related characteristics so unique that the animals become "individualized" and gravitate after death not into this communal pool of consciousness but into the environs (physical or astral) of their human companions, continuing the relationship in their astral bodies, though of course now invisible to their still embodied human friends.

An example of the gradual change in the collective pool of consciousness of rabbits came into my own pool of awareness when, as a teenager learning to drive a car, I began to notice the numbers of rabbits that had been struck and killed by cars on the country roads. Most western roads back in the 1920s were dirt or gravel; few were paved, even in cities, and the speed limit signs usually said, "Thirty Miles an Hour." (I can remember my father telling me that no one ever needed to be in such a hurry that she had to go faster than thirty. Before his death he mentioned, with a bashful smile, that in his new car he had gone eighty. So much for practicing what one preaches!)

To return to the subject of rabbits: I noticed that on roads with a speed limit of forty, many more rabbits had been hit than on roads with a speed limit of thirty. The few roads with a speed limit of forty-five were strewn with rabbits that had failed to estimate accurately the speed of oncoming cars.

As time went on, however, the roads improved and speed limits continued to rise; yet the rabbit body-count began to drop, even along highways with limits of fifty, fifty-five, sixty, although the rabbit population seemed to remain about the same. Even back then, as a teenager, I began to believe that Rabbit, as a group entity, had learned to avoid death by automobile.

It interested me deeply when I learned that Rosicrucianism taught that each species is a group entity with a Group Soul which is intelligent and learns by the collective experiences of its "cells," its individuals. Four years later I learned that Theosophy teaches the same for each species.

In recent years Dr. Rupert Sheldrake of England has put forth a theory of "Morphogenetic Fields" of consciousness, one for each species or subgroup within a species. His theory, quite similar to the concept of Group Souls, has been the object of much discussion and criticism among his peers in the scientific world, as might be expected. He is a careful scientific researcher and his evidence as presented is impressive.

Stories of the spread of a certain knowledge among the living far-flung members of a species during life are abundant: e.g., elephants, horses, termites. I find myself sorely tempted to tell some of them, but this is a book about death, so I'll merely and barely mention *The Hundredth Monkey* (see Bibliography) and a little wasp friend whom I named "Topaz," who has connected me through our mutual respect and friendship with all members of her species *(Polistes vulgaris)* no matter where I may travel, although she is long dead. (Hi, little Topaz. I'm talking about you. Thank you for making all of your relatives friends of mine!)

Pets and Individualization

When I first heard the idea that animals closely associated with people often became "individualized" (with a soul of their own, no longer only a cell of the Group Soul) and at death the individualized animal did not return its life and learning only to the pool of consciousness of its species but kept its astral body and its consciousness close to its human friends, I felt that this must indicate a warping of the natural progress of the animal, taking it away from its cat-path or its dog-development or its horse-evolvement. I was assured, however, that far from being a hindrance to an animal, a close warm association with human beings is an asset, a spiritual benefit to the animal. (This I heard with my usual "put it on the Neutral Shelf" attitude, to wait for further evidence one way or the other.)

Evidence has come along bit by bit through the years. One of the most heartwarming is about my Czechoslovakian friend's little dog in her home near Rio de Janiero.

Albie wrote me that she had walked along the path from her country home to the settling-tank where water for irrigation was diverted from a larger ditch, and somehow while working she slipped in the mud and fell, striking her head on a concrete edge of the settling tank. Unconscious, she lay with her face where the slowly rising water would soon reach and cover it. Just before it did so, friends who had driven up from the city to visit discovered her there and rescued her.

"We found that you were not in the house, so we started looking for you," the friends said. "And we never would have found you if your little dog had not insisted so frantically that we follow him. He led us right to you."

"My little dog?"

"Yes, your little black dog. He saved your life. We arrived just in time; you would have drowned if we had been a bit later. You owe your life to your little dog."

Albie told her friends, "I don't have a dog now. It was a little black dog that you saw? My little black dog was hit by a train two years ago."

Meanwhile the little dog had disappeared. He had done what was necessary and apparently became his invisible astral self again, probably still in the vicinity of the home, however.

The reason I dare to say that is that two psychics who do not know each other have told me that several animals live in my house with me, adding, "but only one that you see." Yes, I have one cat now, but sometimes I think vividly of others and of dogs that we have had in the past. My thinking of them may draw them to stick around, or else maybe their presence causes me to think of them. I was wondering at one time if "Irish," my old blue-eyed Siamese cat, was earth-bound and needed to be "rescued" and helped to go on into the astral plane, but Virginia, a psychic friend and an RN, assured me, "He's all right. He just likes to stay here." I accepted her word for it and have not checked up further on Irish nor on the other invisibles with me.

Euthanasia for Animals

When the owner of an animal feels it necessary to have the animal killed, I believe it is better not to say, "put the animal to sleep" when a child is within hearing distance, because children take words very literally. A child hearing that the old dog was "put to sleep" and finding that the dear old dog never appeared again—and then hearing the mother speak of putting her or the baby to sleep is understandably upset. On the subconscious level such a connection may lie dormant many years but appear at a time of stress as insomnia, a fear of going to sleep.

When I was a little girl I heard my father more than once say about a severely hurt or sick animal, "It will be better to put it out of its misery." I knew he really felt pity for the animal and believed that a quick painless death would save the animal from further suffering. There was no doubt in my mind about his motives. Yet, children that we were and not yet acquainted with much suffering personally, my sister and I absolutely refused to let our Bennie Ralph be helped to die when the beloved cat became very sick. Both parents tried to point out that life was misery for the cat, but we children insisted that he did not seem to be in pain.

"Honeys, he smells so bad," added our mother. Well, yes, but what was a bad smell when it was our dear friend?

And so Bennie Ralph (who had been Betty Ruth until we found out differently) died a lingering death, loved and wept over, and miserable.

Years later, after all my sons had left home, I officiated at the aging and eventual death of the pets they had left behind, four cats and a dog. Ringo, the dog, and two of the cats were sixteen years old together. All three left their bodies that summer, one after the other, and I was emotionally unable to assist them until the very last hours. I cannot even yet say why. I was prepared with a little bottle of chloroform from the sympathetic pharmacist, and ether (to follow a sleep induced gently by the chloroform). I did use these at the last for each of the sick old pets, but why not sooner?

Telling the veterinarian about Ringo, I admitted that I should have had him put Ringo down when he told me that Ringo's kidneys were "shot," but I had promised Ringo that I would bring him back home from the examination. That was a mistake, for I had not realized just how much pain uremia with an acute urinary infection could cause. Ringo died in pain, but I think he knew that I was trying to help him, for he did not turn his head away from the ether and accepted the sleep that relieved him. Later I told the veterinarian, "He died slowly from his disease like a human being. . . ." I was wishing I had not forced him to do so.

Still later, when the vet himself was slowly dying of cancer, too ill to want visitors, I thought of that remark. I wondered if he wished that some merciful doctor might "put him out of his misery," as he so often had done for animals.

There is no fixed rule, because each instance needs to be evaluated individually for the animal and its condition. There are many cases of animals that a veterinarian recommends to be put down, but the animals have been loved and nurtured back to health, and sometimes it is the vet who keeps and cares for an animal whose owner wanted it killed.

We need to remember that an animal, like a human being, has two parts, the physical body and the consciousness, the soul, and these two may not feel the same about dying. The body wants to live, the consciousness wants relief from the body. If we try to imagine what the animal itself would prefer, it might very well be confused and undecided.

Nature, after all, does provide relief in due time. Animals often feel an instinctive desire to wander off when their end-time is approaching. They seek a place of quiet where they can lie down and simply let go of life. Perhaps they do not do this consciously as much as from a vagueness of mind, but the result may be the same.

Shep, the faithful dog of an elderly couple, had been unwell for some weeks and wandered away from the country home. Hal went in search of Shep, found him, carried him home. A second time Shep disappeared, and again Hal searched until he found the dog and brought him home. Shep was too weak to go a third time. He lay moaning in the house, and Hal was distraught.

"I don't know why animals have to suffer like that," he exclaimed, close to tears.

Purposely I let my voice become a bit sharp. "Well, you are forcing him to suffer. He wanted to just go away and die, and you kept bringing him back."

This ruse worked as I hoped that it would. Hal became calmer, accepting his part. He allowed his wife and me to carry Shep outside to a little shed where Mary and I offered Shep a wad of cotton saturated with ether while we talked to him and stroked him. His moaning became fainter and then ceased. I left more ether by his nose, we covered him, and returned to the house where we found Hal calm and sad but composed. I believe that he needed an outside voice to tell him that it was all right to let Shep die, that he did not need to continue seeking means to stall off death to prove his love and caring. Our culture has programmed us to feel that love is proved by prolonging life, whether or not life is bearable.

Edith, whom I mentioned earlier, told me that when she had to have her dear old dog put down, she put the dog into the vet's arms and he started to carry the dog down the hall. The dog whined and turned its head back toward Edith and gave her such a look that she could not tell me of it without tears. "It was the look of one who had been betrayed," she said. "I can't forget that look."

Two women friends, one a nurse, also had to have their dog put down. June told me that they informed the veterinarian that they wanted to stay with their pet while he gave the injection. So they were beside the dog, talking to it and stroking it as the drug took effect. I believe that this closeness in the last moments of life is better for the animal, and I feel also that it is better for the human beings. It relieves them of the guilt that they may otherwise feel, although it does require courage. As I said, however, each case is individual.

In all three of these cases the love between dog and human beings was such that I would not be at all surprised if a psychic saw the dog in its astral body still with its family of humans.

It would be a good project for research if a sympathetic veterinarian could enlist the cooperation of a reliable psychic and the two could check up on some of the animals that have to be put down, discovering the main pathways for the animal souls after being freed from the body, and in fact rechecking the accuracy of the concept of Group Souls and Pools of Consciousness—and, most especially, *learning whether the animals appreciate such a termination* of their physical life—that is, whether this is an unnatural and abnormal act, even though motivated by sympathy and "common sense."

If Not Death, What?

If the answer is found generally to be against euthanasia for the animal, the best alternatives need to be discovered and promulgated. Just taking the unwanted animal out to some isolated spot and "dumping" it is certainly not a humane act, leaving the pet betrayed, hoping against hope for its family's return to get it, unused to seeking its own food, slowly starving. Far better to pay the small fee to have the pet put down than to force it to suffer the long slow death of both body and trust.

On the other hand, when I was preparing to move a few miles from my old home to a new place, I considered whether my three cats would care for town life after the freedom of the country and might actually be in danger from town traffic in the new home. At a reading with Nan Taylor, our ESP instructor, I asked Demetrius through her whether I should have two of the cats "gently put to death" to save them from the trauma of the move and of city living. I felt that there was a shocked pause before Demetrius answered, "Why not take them with you? If they do not like it, they will leave." And I felt the rest of the message unspoken: Animals do have a right to live and gain experience.

Therefore, I took the cats with me. The Siamese, "Irish," adjusted rather quickly, as I had known he would, but the two younger, wilder females had a much longer orientation period. When they finally did feel at ease in the new place, Feather became a contented house cat, but Rattle-kit was a roving spirit, repeatedly making her way back to the old home, where the new residents would notice her and phone me. I would go and bring her back, but in a few weeks this scenario would be repeated. After the third time, I knew that she "will leave if she does not like it," just as Demetrius had known; his words had warned me of the possibility. For a week before she left the fourth time she became more affectionate than ever and showed in every possible cat-manner that she held no hard feelings toward me. So when she disappeared I sent my good wishes after her and let her go free—probably to live only a relatively short life, trading security for freedom by her own choice (just as some human beings do).

Old Irish died the next spring. Feather tried to take his place on the bed and in my life, but in a few years she died, possibly from poison. Her body was near the house and seemed uninjured. I knew that some of the neighbors disliked roving cats and felt great anger at people who brought their unwanted pets to this subdivision to "dump" them, hoping that one of the residents would adopt the discarded animals. Very, very few ever did. Each family either had its own pets or did not want any at all, and they resented the controlling attitude of the former pet-owners who would attempt to foist their unwanted pets on other persons. It was not unusual for such a resentful person to poison or shoot a cat or dog that came to investigate a garbage barrel. At any rate, Feather made it almost home before she died. I was glad for that.

Animal Souls After Death

Three rather different stories of animals who were seen or contacted after dying follow:

The first was obtained at a releasement session of a client in whom we found the consciousness of a British big-game hunter. The hunter was reluctant to divulge much information about himself—I had the impression that his death had been due to some carelessness that he felt ashamed to admit—and he would not give his name; he allowed me to address him simply as "Sir." After coming out of my client at my request but still speaking through her voice, he described seeing a wide beautiful area and saw himself surrounded by animals: "Many animals—running! All running!"

"Are they frightened? Are they running away from you?"

"They are happy; they are just running and happy," he said.

It interested me that he had no desire now to kill them again. Instead he felt the joyfulness of the animals whose bodies he had taken pleasure in killing. His desire to control was gone as was the animals' fear.

A second animal story that ends happily is the story of "Humdee," the pet and companion of my friend Freda. When she went to Saudi Arabia with her husband to work there, she left Humdee in the care of a friend in Maryland. It was a wrench for her to leave the dog, and Humdee let it be known that she did not want to be parted from her mistress. Worse, after a short time Humdee disappeared, and Freda, filled with guilt for not having taken Humdee with her, was sure that the dog had been caught and used as a tortured experimental animal in some laboratory.

So keen was Freda's remorse (although I wondered if any dog would have been welcome in Saudi Arabia) that I asked a friend to channel in hypnosis for me, to try to get information about Humdee and find out her situation.

"She is an adventurous spirit, like her mistress. She wandered away," we were told by the entity who located Humdee. "She is a happy spirit."

So we knew that Humdee was dead but is now happy. I asked specifically if she had been used in a laboratory and was told "No." My intuitive impression, although I did not ask, was that she had been hit by a car.

In the third animal story it was Freda who channeled a consciousness that was in the vicinity of the new house that the family had bought. Freda had the feeling that something dark was hovering around the place. When we contacted it in hypnosis, it said it was a dog—a dog that had been trapped inside the former house that had burned down. The dog was earth-bound, feeling that it was supposed to stay in this place and not knowing where else to go. It was not a pet but was not vicious; it had a rather colorless personality, bored, sad, and lonely. I asked the Group Soul of dogs to come for it and take care of it, not knowing exactly what instructions from me would be best for it. (In conversing with it I reminded it to put its *thoughts* into Freda's mind and she would speak the thoughts aloud to me. This telepathic method in hypnosis makes communication simple and easy.)

When I mentioned to Karen, a hypnotherapist friend in Santa Fe, New Mexico, that I was writing about animal deaths and would welcome contributions she said, "Oh, I have a good one for you!" Here is what she wrote:

Chanté's Farewell

When my two cats and I moved into a guesthouse surrounded by towering ponderosa pines in the mountains of Santa Fe, we soon discovered the guardian of the property: an enormous woolly old malamute named Chanté.

Usually fearful of being alone, I was never bothered by the remoteness, as Chanté abandoned her doghouse each evening for my front porch. I even bought her an old wool coat for a mat, which she loved. Too old and fat to play any more, she still managed a "Woof!" and tail wags for greetings. But she truly belonged heart and soul to Jack, who had just married my dearest friend, Eva. Chanté and Jack took daily long walks to the mailbox. In the summers she would sometimes naughtily submerge herself in the small smelly pond nearby, creating real waves at home when she returned.

After about a year I married my fiance and moved into Santa Fe. Only when I visited my dear friends would Chanté and I renew our bond. She seemed more and more ancient and slow, and didn't even seem to register my presence but slept in her woolly cocoon of fur.

About two years after I had moved, Jack and Eva invited me as their guest to an opera benefit in Lamy, near Santa Fe. I was to meet them there at 5:30. Around 3:00 that afternoon I became so deeply sleepy that I just had to take a nap (a rare occasion for me). As I slept, I suddenly "saw" Chanté, in her favorite spot outside the guesthouse. She just stood and stared intensely into my eyes for a long minute. Then the next second she transformed into her younger self about one or two years old: she was slender, beautiful, racing about, begging me to come and play with her . . . her joy was obvious! Then the "dream" evaporated; I awoke bewildered, even amused.

Later, when I joined the crowd at the opera party, I found Eva but didn't see Jack. Eva explained sadly, "Jack will come later. He found his Chanté in a coma-like state this afternoon; when he couldn't waken her, he called the vet. Chanté was put sleep before she could suffer. . . ."

My shock was doubled as I suddenly recalled my strange "dream" that afternoon. "Oh, I'm so sorry! What time did all this take place?" I asked. Eva answered, "Chanté was put to sleep around 3:00." Later that evening I shared my amazing story with them both, believing that Chanté somehow wanted me to.

Every time that I recall this incident, I ask myself again, "Why did she contact *me*, and show me that she was healed and renewed?" Although no answer has ever appeared, few experiences have truly honored me more than Chanté's farewell.

P.S. About three years after Chanté's death, Jack, 75 years old, also left this earth. I, for one, am certain of their reunion!

Such appearances of a deceased *human* being to a loved survivor have been reported many times but less often the appearance of a *non-human* spirit. Perhaps it is that the expectation of such an apparition is hoped for when the one dead is human, but is not even thought of in the case of a deceased animal. Or it may be that there are many such cases of animals returning in the astral body to say good-bye, but their human friends have hesitated to mention the contact. I am glad to have Karen's experience here to share with all persons who may have had a similar one, either in a "dream" or merely as a strong feeling.

As for the transformation of old feeble Chanté into a frolicsome puppy, that type of change is "par" for the astral course. Remember, desire and thought are the astral tools. Without deliberate thinking, Chanté undoubtedly felt the lightness and joy of release from her old heavy body and her emotions became her elixir of puppyhood! Why did she appear to Karen and not to her loved master, Jack? I believe that the reason may involve some technical things like "polarity" or perhaps simply the state of the conscious mind of the receiver of such a contact. Karen's mind was sleeping and receptive. Jack's mind, on the other hand, was awake and grieving. Jack need not have grieved.

Animals in the Laboratory

There is much emotion on both sides of the argument about the use of animals in medical schools and pharmacological experiments. The basic difference in attitude seems to be one of focus: the research-oriented workers are usually the calm, dispassionate type who focus on the results of the experiments, which are largely those of economic or medical value to human beings; whereas the persons we might call life-oriented are sensitive to forms of life aside from the human and feel not only the physical discomforts and pains of the experimental animals but their emotions as well: from boredom to despair to terror.

It is regrettable that there is so little communication between the two groups, neither side willing to listen to the other, each side covertly or overtly contemptuous of the other; one side calling the other "bleeding hearts," who are calling them in return hard-hearted insensitive exploiters of sentient living creatures.

It is true that animal experiments have provided much valuable information for new drugs and household commodities; it is also true that many experiments have been unnecessary or unnecessarily cruel. It is true that in medical schools some of the experiments are careless of the animals' welfare during their captivity in cages and careless of the animals' pain and fear during the experiments. Much could be done, much needs to be done, to improve the general

conditions concerning animal experimentation, starting
with the attitudes of the researchers toward nonhuman life-
forms.

Students required to perform painful experiments on
animals are deeply shocked more often than the instructors
are aware. Most students simply grit their teeth and go ahead
with the assigned work. But after one laboratory session
working on frogs, one of the few young women in my
medical class began to make the rounds of the entire large
room, pausing at each wastebasket—checking, she said, to be
sure that no live frogs had been discarded to die slowly. My
high regard for her rose higher after that little incident—of
which she seemed almost apologetic. My own memories of
some of the animal experiments in both graduate school and
medical school are still so painful to me that even now I turn
away from them mentally. It is very difficult for me now to
write those paragraphs above. But I feel that it is important
that these things be mentioned in this book about death and
about the distress and pain that may precede the relief of
death. Experiments can be made as gentle as possible. An
example is:

"Hexa Everlasting"

One experiment in graduate school required the removal
of the pituitary gland of salamanders, to show the students
the relation between the gland and the behavior of the
pigment cells in the salamanders' skin. When the pigment
cells were tightly contracted, the color of the lizard-like
animals was very pale; when the pigment cells were expanded, the color became dark. The salamanders controlled
their color through the hormone of the pituitary gland.

Anesthetizing each little six-inch salamander with a few
drops of Chloretone in the water, I operated carefully on
several animals and watched as they returned to consciousness. There was no trouble—not until Salamander No. Six.

Then I accidentally damaged an artery in the operative area. I could not get the bleeding stopped. Sadly I laid the little limp body aside and began to clean up the instruments—when I saw Number Six begin to stir. She was alive! After giving her time to recuperate a while, I attempted the operation again, but alas, the damaged artery began to bleed again, and for a second time I regretfully laid the poor little body aside.

Ah, but a second time the little body began to move—again it had come back to life. This time I refused to do any more unnatural procedures to it and decided to keep Number Six as a pet. I named her "Hexa Everlasting"—"Number Six Everlasting." I kept her until she died by herself in a night-time adventure after escaping from her aquarium. She had become very dark: "The operation was successful—but the patient (eventually) died." But don't we all, eventually?

The Animals' Higher Awareness Has Free Will

The above was a totally new idea to me when, through my co-worker Linda, Master Ching was discussing this subject of animal experiments. I had spoken of my decades-long grief and sadness at the memories of some of the experiments that I had been required to perform, and mentioned other cruelties that sadistic psychotics and criminals commit, acts that are warped and unnatural and cannot be considered "good" or "right" or "decent."

"Yes. Even as I am—" he began, and at the words my mind flew to the meaning: Just as my co-workers who have seen him have said, Master Ching is "very high, very beautiful, with wide clear wisdom."

I felt that he sensed my recognition, for he paused a moment, and then went on quietly, repeating, "Even as I am, I too have struggled. A pattern of cruelty has developed. You are not and never have been a part of that pattern. We on this side are working to control and change it, just as you on that side are working, and we are glad for all the help you can give. As for the experiments, have people learned from them what they sought to learn? If so, then the life of the animal has not been in vain and it has accomplished what it came into earth-life to do."

I thought I heard him but was not sure I had heard rightly.

"Do you mean that the animal was *willing* to become an experimental animal in a laboratory?"

"Oh, my, yes," said Master Ching quietly. "Animals have free will."

In these few sentences he relieved me of a great deal of my guilt and sorrow about my own past lab activities and explained a great deal about the entire subject of cruelties: first, that the pattern of *cruelty is not part of the Great Plan* (as implied by persons who state that all is as it should be in God's Plan) but is an aberration that needs to be controlled and then changed, and second, that animal souls as well as human souls have the wonderful and dangerous gift of free-will. Like human souls, however, it seems that they may offer to do something to benefit other lives and when the time comes to fulfill that resolution on the earth-plane they find that it entails unexpected pain—just as did the mother who chose to die in the gas chamber with her little son, fulfilling her own soul's desire to do something to help others.

And so we are given a new respect and reverence for "lower" lives, a respect that Albert Schweitzer had learned and had tried to transmit to his fellow workers in his motto, "Reverence for All Life." He meant this literally! I still smile at the memory of his interchange with a reporter to whom he was talking in his compound in Africa. The mosquitoes were numerous, and the reporter reached to swat one that had alighted on Schweitzer's arm.

"That was MY mosquito," objected Schweitzer.

We cannot all leap at once to the height of reverence for all life that Schweitzer had attained, but we certainly can become aware of the beauty and sacredness of the Great Plan that includes so many marvelous life-forms besides the one species of *Homo sapiens*. We can put aside our arrogant feelings of superiority and, like many tribes that live close to Nature, accept other living creatures as our siblings and cousins, as "all God's Chillen," or "all our relatives," as the Native Americans say.

12

AND ON BEYOND

Life and Death and Thoughts about Both

YOU READERS WHO TALK TO YOUR HOUSE PLANTS or your garden flowers, you farmers who send thoughts of encouragement and pride to your crops or suffer with their thirst in times of drought, do you feel that the plants communicate with you sometimes? Well, they are living creatures, too, of course. You will be interested in the remarkable book, *The Secret Life of Plants* (see Bibliography) which provides scientific evidence, with electronics and graphs, that plants sense "telepathically" what a person is thinking or feeling toward them.

And why are we surprised by things like this? When we try to define "life" in the physiological sense, we say that life is manifested by motion, respiration, reproduction, intake of food with digestion and elimination, and conversion of the energy of food into other forms of energy. It would certainly seem that all these processes and activities require a source of intelligence. So now we come closer to trying to define "Life" in the total sense. Then where does Death enter the picture?

Death receives the physical body eventually, of course; that is intended to be recycled. This does not mean that we should not deal respectfully with the bodies of our dead. It simply means that we clothe the dead body, surround it with

220

flowers, have a ceremony in its honor, and then bury or burn it while continuing to love and cherish the livingness of the mind and heart-feelings that once used that body. But the energy that used that body, the energies it contained—the energy of motion, of warmth, of reproduction, and all the other manifestations of energy—are now absent, and the form (of plant or animal or human being) lies slack and lifeless.

Where have the energies gone? Physics tells us that the energy can not be destroyed; it can only be transformed from one form into another. And what about the energies of thought, of feeling? The tremendous energy of desire?

I believe that the science of the non-material mind is a separate science from the science of the physical brain and its sensory and motor parts. Death is an aspect of the physical and physiological sciences, whose books of information and knowledge are on the lowest two shelves of "the Bookcase of Human Knowledge." The books about mind, psychological processes, emotions, thought, are on the next higher shelf, and those concerned with spiritual laws and Life in the highest sense are on the top shelf. Death, then, is way down there near the bottom, not up here—not up here where *we* are, our minds, our livingness and intelligence and that of our fellow "mortals" on the Earth: animals, plants, seeds; to a certain degree, also even minerals, crystals, molecules. . . .

Science has called portions of these shelves *Kingdoms:* the Animal Kingdom, the Human Kingdom, and so on. We discover that above the Human Kingdom is a Spiritual Kingdom, like a graduate school for souls outgrowing the limitations of human fears and angers. It is in the Spiritual Kingdom that a human soul may become a Teacher or a Master, training the less evolved spiritual Guides to assist us who still struggle in the difficulties of human physical life, and themselves helping humanity when asked.

And again, where is Death in this scheme? Not here, not in the Spiritual Kingdom.

Well, in extremely rare instances, Death may appear, but only when chosen by a being that prefers extinction (of the individuality) to the long hard path of karmic retribution and rebalancing. I have encountered only two such cases in all my hundreds of sessions, and both of those were of dark non-human entities encountered during Releasement sessions. I felt that in these two instances there was true Death, self-chosen. For me it was an awesome realization. The first entity, however, said that obliteration would be preferable to the long-continued karmic suffering and hard labor, and as it "melted" into the Light, it murmured, "It is happening. . . . It is peace. . . ." Even in these circumstances, Death is found to be peace. Suppose that a Hitler, having condemned himself to suffer everything that every one of his victims suffered, might choose Death, to escape that nearly endless succession of blighted incarnations. He knows that he has free will to choose, but after choosing Death "he" would be gone—no feeling, no mind, nothing left to his individuality.

The laws of karma, however, offer different ways in which debts may be balanced. Sufferings inflicted need not be expiated entirely by suffering the same things in a future time. Much can be balanced by selfless outpouring of the life into helping others who happen to be less fortunate at the moment.

Two Genealogies for Each Person

It will be easy to perceive by now that each of us has a long personal history of intertwined threads, perhaps conceived as a double-helix as in the DNA molecule. One thread is the ages-long heritage of the *physical body*, going back through the generations, the source of much interesting research for many persons and the reason for the careful record-keeping of groups like the Jews, the Mormons, the Quakers, and others. Genes inherited from our physical ancestors determine the color of our eyes, the type of body-build, the facial features, etc. We say, "Your son looks just like you," or "You have your mother's eyes." Certain psychological characteristics and susceptibilities to certain diseases may also be inherited.

The other thread of the double-helix is our *personal past-life history*, not dependent on any other being. It is composed of the chain of our own past thoughts, feelings, and deeds, our responses to the events of each of our previous lives, and contains within each of these the *cause* of a future event. The law of karma is simply the outworking of our own past deeds.

As such, karma is not punitive, it is simply the result of our own thinking and activities; it is the Law of Just Compensation, the reaping of what we have sown. We learn from our mistakes as well as from our wise decisions and courageous acts, and as we learn, our character matures and becomes ever more strong, wise, and clear until eventually, after many lives, we are strong, wise, and saintly enough to grow out of the Human Kingdom and enter (psychospiritually) the Spiritual Kingdom. This promotion may not occur until after many more lifetimes or it may occur at any time during the present physical life.

It is a growth that makes a profound alteration in the person's attitudes and reactions to life situations, usually gradual, occasionally abrupt. Friends and relatives may wonder what has produced such a major change in the person. The person may look the same outwardly and appear to be still a member of the Human Kingdom, but inwardly the former "merely human" traits have been altered beyond recognition. The old lama in Kipling's novel,

Kim, said, "When I was a man, . . ." speaking of that former
time and former personality. Paul, the Apostle, spoke of
putting off the "old" man and the "natural" man: "Put off
your old nature which belongs to your former manner of life
and is corrupt through deceitful lusts, and be renewed in the
spirit of your minds, and put on the new nature, created after
the likeness of God in true righteousness and holiness" (I
Corinth. 4:22-24).

Dr. Denning's "Dead" Host

In response to my request for an account of one or more
of her interesting sessions or experiences about death, Dr.
Hazel Denning took time from her busy schedule to write the
following illuminating report:

> For a number of years I had a class which studied all
> aspects of the paranormal world. We were using one of the
> very sensitive (psychic) members to answer questions for
> anything the group wanted to explore. One evening she
> was interpreting the dreams of each individual.
> Our host described a dream of standing with arms
> wide, gazing at a huge forest on fire. He was in awe at the
> beauty and magnificence of it. She told him it indicated that
> he was on the verge of a really important adventure in his
> life, and it was good. After the meeting she told me it was
> foretelling his transition: that he was going to die even
> before the next monthly meeting. Two weeks later, while
> driving with his wife, he suffered a heart attack at the wheel
> of his car and ran into a fire hydrant. He died instantly; his
> wife was not seriously hurt.
> At the next meeting our psychic (in trance) reported
> that our host was present and sitting in a certain chair. We
> all acknowledged his presence, though no one saw him. We
> asked him questions, and he carried on a lengthy conversa-
> tion with us, through her. He reported that he was free to

come and go as he pleased and was doing a lot of exploring, and spending time with his wife so she would not be so lonely. He said that he was being given three months (by our time) to do whatever he pleased, and then he would be given an assignment on his plane.

Numerous interesting things happened during the three months. One morning his wife found a yellow rose on her porch, still fresh with dew. At the next meeting he asked her how she liked it and told her he had sent it. Later I asked him how he did it. He said he had to work at it, but he had impressed a child going to school to pick it and put it on the porch. There were no yellow roses in the immediate neighborhood.

At one of our meetings we had a guest who was also very psychic. He came in, sat down, looked puzzled, and after some hesitation asked, "Who is that gentleman over in that chair?" It was the chair we always left unoccupied. We asked him to describe what he saw, and he gave us a complete description of our unseen host. Our special guest seemed baffled by the actions of our spirit: "I never before saw a ghost wipe his glasses. He was laughing along with the rest of you and took off his glasses, pulled his handkerchief from his pocket, and wiped them." This brought another burst of laughter from all of us, for we had seen our former host do that many times. He loved a joke and always removed his glasses and wiped them after laughing really hard.

One evening he asked if we would like to hear what it was like to die and promised that if I would bring a tape recorder to the next meeting he would describe his transition. Of course we all agreed that we would appreciate such information.

First of all he paid high tribute to his wife for preparing him for this great experience. He had had no interest in metaphysics all the years when he had been a successful real estate man. But his wife constantly bought more books about it. She had noted that all of a sudden he was reading her books. His interest had started three months before his transition. She was delighted, of course, at his enthusiastic responses to what he was reading and they spent considerable time discussing it. On this evening, he said he wanted to thank her for encouraging him to study, because that was what had made his transition so beautiful. He explained that being prepared made all the difference in the world in the experience.

He had died expecting an afterlife. He had been a good man, honest and with integrity in his business always. He explained no words could do justice to the experience of transition, but it was like being catapulted into the most brilliant and beautiful light you could imagine. (Our psychic who was relaying his message said that he was euphoric and was only frustrated because he could not adequately convey the magnificence of the experience.) After that initial thrust into the light, there were light beings who came to welcome him and explain how he was to proceed and conduct himself.

After about three months he announced that he would not be with us again, for he was now ready to take up some responsibilities in his dimension. Also, he said it was not good for his wife to be so dependent on our monthly meetings, for she was living for those meetings and that was interfering with the work she should be doing. He told her to let go of the fear she still carried about driving, and just get in her car and go. We all thanked him for visiting us every meeting and wished him well in his life "over there." He never came again.

Hazel Denning, who has been called "the Mother of Past-life Research," has been active in past-life research and therapy for over forty years. I quote her report at length because of all the very significant details it contains: First, that some newly deceased souls are free for a period to come and go, not earth-bound nor yet "gone to the Light." Second, that souls who have reached a certain stage of spiritual development are not merely expected to learn but also to take on "assignments" in the astral world at their particular level or dimension. And third, that before they become too much involved in that assignment they may still be able, in the near-earth plane, to affect embodied persons' thoughts and "impress" them to think or do certain things—as the child was "impressed" to pick a rose and later to leave it on someone's porch. The man who died said he spent time with his wife, trying to comfort her—although, because he was invisible, she seemed to be unaware of his attempts to "impress" her with his presence, living instead for the monthly meetings when, through the psychic as a channel, she could talk directly to her husband.

Assignments After Death

One time I asked a psychic friend, Carroll, if my mother were earth-bound. She died in 1946, but at times I thought I had felt her presence rather clearly. Carroll meditated a moment and then said, drawing a sketch on a paper, "No, she is free and is working in two levels, the Field of Education and the Field of Service. When she is down at the level of Service, she is close to earth. She just likes to check in on you now and then."

Then Carroll drew another circle higher on the page. "Your father works in two levels also, in the Field of Education and in the Field of Knowledge. I've never found anyone before who worked in the Field of Knowledge."

"I can easily understand that," I told her. "He was interested in everything and had knowledge of many things."

"And because he also works in the Field of Education, he is in contact with your mother at that level," she continued.

It was a pleasant, warm feeling to have an idea of what my parents were doing, busy and useful and happy, not simply sleeping or harping around!

I was told what my own assignment is to be, and in a most unusual manner:

While I was doing a Rescue session (with Cynthia, a co-worker, in hypnosis and the rest of our group present) we found first a girl of thirteen who had voluntarily remained earth-bound, trying to find her grown brother, after dying on a ship that had been sunk. He, too, was found—searching for her! Other souls from the ship also came at our call and followed the girl and her brother into the Light. But one sailor remained obdurate.

"His name's Bartholomew or Bart," said Cynthia in hypnosis. "He's trying to take his bones with him. He won't go to the Light. . . . Broken, nasty old bones. You can't convince him. I don't think he'll come. He has his sword and his bones."

The group of us began to suppress chuckles. I launched into an explanation to Bartholomew of the advantages of leaving the drowning scene and going to the Light.

"Hush, hush, old woman! I want my bones," he interrupted. The titters grew louder. "There are people coming, picking up my bones. They have no respect for the dead."

Some laughs broke out, in spite of efforts at control.

"Listen to me, Bartholomew. Those people are simply curious. The body after death is no good. It needs to be recycled. Look inside yourself: How do you look?"

"It's ugly."

"Wouldn't you rather have a clean bright self in the Light?"

"Do I need my sword?"

"No, not your old sword. Here, I'll give you a new one, a sword of freedom and liberation."

"It's not rusty. What is it made of?"

"It's made of blue light; with it you can get rid of things like hate and fear."

"How do I protect myself?"

"With this blue sword of freedom. You don't need the old sword. Remember, this is not a sword of killing or destruction, it is a sword of liberation."

"Can I keep the new sword? What about my bones?"

There was a burst of uninhibited laughter from the group. Bart did not seem to hear it. He asked more questions about the place to which he would go if he left this place, wondering if his drinking buddies would be there. "You said 'friends,'" he reminded me.

"Not drinking buddies, but people like you. Put out of yourself the old ways and the alcohol addiction. . . . Tell me, whom did you love? Or even a pet, a dog, a cat?"

There was a pause. Then, "I had a little kitten."

"Have you seen the kitten there? Call her now."

"Okay, I'll call my kitten. Then can I put a curse on the guy who is messing with my bones?" (Hilarious guffaws.)

Stifling my own laughter I said, "No, he's just interested—he's a diver."

"Everyone wants my bones. Can I take my new sword and my kitten?"

"I am going to invite someone who cares about Bart to please come to escort him to his own rightful home."

"I have my kitten. . . . [pause] Do you know who's here? The old nun from the orphanage. I didn't think she liked me."

"She cares about you. I asked for someone who *cared* about you to come."

"She looks just the same. Is she going to hit me? She used to whack me all the time."

"Oh, no. Sister, why don't you say something to Bart?"

"She's telling me about this lovely place. . . . I have to go back to school. She said I could take my kitten. I have to learn to use my sword correctly. . . . She says I need to apologize to you. I'm sorry I was unkind."

"You didn't know. It's all right."

"She said you are going to come and teach at the school."
(Oh? I am? Well. . . .)

"Not until next semester or so: not this term."

(Oh!) "I'll be glad to see you, when I come. Good-bye, Bart."

So, you see, I already have my assignment!

How Do We Prepare for Our Death?

Several steps or stages are easily discernible, sketched out by the deceased host in Dr. Denning's account: first, a frank *consideration of non-physical realities* and invisible realms of conscious existence. This may imply conversations with interested friends, finding books on the subjects, etc.

Second, or maybe first, an acceptance, either mental or emotional, based on either conscience or religion, that to be ready to die implies as much *clearing of the personality and character* as possible *before* any direct face-to-face encounter with death. Then, no matter when that encounter may occur, we can feel ready and at ease. This stage may include any and all means of purification, from apologizing to persons we have injured in the past, to yogic approaches, religious rituals, meditations, and other self-chosen or suggested methods of what is now called Self-improvement.

Third, the development, deliberate or intuitive, of the attitude of "listening" for higher guidance, and then learning not to disobey that guidance. It may help us if we visualize a wise guardian angel or mentally communicate with a revered teacher or relative who is deceased, and "listen" for answers and advice.

Fourth, to develop, consciously and purposefully, the broad understanding that *all* forms of life are precious in the Universe, that *all* living creatures (plant, animal, human) are miraculous manifestations of life in physical bodies, and that all physical bodies are intended to be temporary houses for the immortal indwelling spiritual life. This means that the color of the fur or hair or eyes or skin of a physical body is of minor importance and that the "color" of the soul, the deep character, is what is most important.

Fifth, to broaden our understanding of others—not into a rigid harsh preaching of "goodness" to those one feels are lacking goodness, but into a wide-spreading, all-embracing compassion and gentleness toward those felt to be lacking in the traits needed, with patience and yet firmness in our attitudes when with them: firm toward our own conscience and chosen directions, patient and gentle toward others. Nor should we allow ourselves to become unduly upset by any earthly hardships that may fall, even upon those dear to the heart who seem to be straying away from the good path. We may pray or meditate for them, but realize that we are to permit others to have free will—freedom even to make mistakes, trusting the Law that says, "Eventually they will return."

During the period of preparing ourselves for death, it is helpful to watch consciously the stages as we are dropping off into natural sleep. But this is of less importance than to clear the character as much as possible, looking frankly and honestly at Death as part of Life and putting aside old religious or superstitious fears. We need to live well in the present, using common sense and foresight, and valuing each day and hour as opportunity to appreciate and enjoy, to learn and serve. As my own Higher Self advised me, "Keep a-chuggin'."

A poem (author unknown) is appropriate if one thinks of the "unknown morrow" as death:

GUIDANCE

Child of my love, fear not the unknown morrow:
Dread not the new demand Life makes of thee:
Thy ignorance doth hold no cause for sorrow
Since what thou knowest not is known to Me.

One step thou seest; then go forward boldly.
One step is far enough for faith to see.
Take that, and thy next duty shall be told thee,
For step by step the Lord is leading thee.

Stand not in fear, thine adversaries counting:
Dare every peril save to disobey.
Thou shalt march on, all obstacles surmounting.
For I, the Lord, will open up the way.

Wherefore, go gladly to the task assigned thee,
Having my promise: needing nothing more
Than just to know, wheree'er the future find thee,
In all thy journeyings I go before.

Now We Are Ready

So, now that we have prepared ourselves mentally and
spiritually, we realize that our deceased friends and relatives
are waiting for us, patiently but with expectation and joy.
Who are they all? Those whom we have loved and admired,
and those who have loved or admired us, even without our
awareness, either in the physical life or in the mental realm—
the authors of books we have found valuable, the teachers
and professors who have influenced us, the persons whose
lives a smile or a sentence of ours has touched. Such contacts,
even brief and seemingly trivial, may establish a bond. So we

list our closely held souls of the present or the past and expect to meet them when we enter their realm.

Then once more we review our list of omissions and fill up those emptinesses as best we can: the letter not written, the apology not offered, the tenderness we were too embarrassed to express. And during all this we may begin to feel a nostalgia for something not quite definable. Is it that we are homesick for the Bright World and want to go Home? Or is it that we feel a deep love for this dear familiar physical world and the friends and relatives here?

This is almost a natural stage for we are in both worlds at once, with one foot in each, so to speak. We just need to be patient with ourselves; take a friend or the family to dinner; attend a concert; read a funny story; see a comedy—just have fun. Then take a long soak in a tub of warm water, go to bed, and sleep a long deep sleep—and next morning get up, stretch, breathe deeply, smile at the face in the mirror, and begin to "chug" again. It is all right. We have simply been vaporizing our old superstitious ideas about death, that's all. We need to allow a little time for those vapors to dissipate in the free air of Eternity. Let us be grateful for having had the wondrous gift of physical life in the beautiful Earth Plane as long as we have. And now we are ready for the Transition into the next world whenever it may be the Right Time for us.

We do not know when the Right Time may come. One of my co-workers, Charlene Smith, RN, writes of a time when almost everyone thought she was dying. This is her account:

> In February, 1995, I went to the Emergency Room of our local hospital (in Delta, Colorado) because of a severe asthmatic attack that progressed to respiratory failure. After I felt the relief of being where I could get help, I realized I was getting weaker. I heard one of the nurses say, "The muscles just can't do any more," and someone else said,

"The medicine should be doing something by now if it's going to."

I remember thinking, "I don't think I'm going to die, but I'd better say a little prayer." So I said silently, "Thank you for my happy life, and please forgive my sins." That was the last I remember until I woke up on a ventilator in the I.C.U. (Intensive Care Unit).

Several family members were there, and I seemed to know what had happened and what was going on, although I was concerned when I couldn't talk (because of the tracheal tube). I was alert and indicated I needed to communicate by writing. My writing was difficult to read but did make sense.

The family didn't stay long, and after they left I had an amazing experience. I saw an angel (or a spirit guide—maybe they are the same).

At the foot of my bed near the wall and up higher than the floor there was a tall slender figure that looked very sedate—almost stern. The figure was pale and was dressed in a white gown and cream-colored robe. It did not seem to be either male or female.

I thought, "I'm hallucinating" and deliberately turned away. I didn't see the figure when I turned away, and thought, "If this is an hallucination, I should still see it (no matter where I look)."

When I looked back, the figure was still there, and it spoke—not with a voice or even like in telepathy. It was like a thought that seemed to fill the whole space, "We're going to leave you now. You'll be all right on your own." I do not know if this was an editorial "we." I only saw one being.

This happened after I was awake and alert. The doctor said there was a period of only about five minutes when I was not breathing before I was given an anesthetic and intubated. Also I never felt that I had "left my body."

For these reasons I do not believe this was a near-death experience but was an angel-encounter. But I do believe the message was real because when I previously had contact (in hypnosis) with a spirit guide, I had been told that I was doing all right on my own, but if I ever needed help, he would be there.

With that in mind, the above message made sense. I had been given help when it was needed, things were going to be all right now, so I didn't need to worry. I realized that if and when I needed help again, it would be there.

As soon as I received the message, the being disappeared, and I had a feeling of love and peace.

When Charlene told me more over the phone, she added that she had always feared a possible death in *status asthmaticus* but had found that this experience, bringing her very close to death, was "not bad at all," to her surprise. She said that she no longer dreads a severe asthmatic attack nor fears dying from one.

The ramifications of the subjects of dying and death spread so widely that it is hard to decide where to place limits for a book like this one. The subject of spiritual advisors and spirit guides and angelic beings, for instance, includes death situations but also includes life experiences!

Much exists in the invisible realms of which we know as yet very little and which we may sweep aside as unimportant because it is invisible. This is hardly a scientific attitude! Far better is the open attitude expressed by one of my professors in medical school, when he remarked that when an infant or child was ill, restless, or delirious, a prayer by the mother or father often soothed the child into restful sleep, "We do not know why." This was way back in 1939 or 1940, at Tulane. After many decades of passing over such relationships, some medical schools are now beginning to take them seriously and perform experiments with prayer. (I might add that the experimenters need to be aware that any deep mental bias of their own will inevitably affect the outcome, whether they "believe" or "disbelieve" in the efficacy of such techniques as prayer, Therapeutic Touch, etc.). Tennyson's line of poetry is still true, "More things are wrought by prayer than this world dreams of."

And so, as we near our own Transition, it is probably a very good idea to do as Charlene did and "say a little prayer." Hers was short and to the point. She commented that it interested her to realize that she had not prayed to live nor even to be relieved of the respiratory distress but simply offered gratitude for her "happy life" and "please forgive my sins." Knowing Charlene for many years, I know that her life was not always happy. There was widowhood, there were accidents, there was the withdrawal of a close family member, and so on. Nor did she have any "sins" of which I was aware. But her little prayer was a good pattern for all of us.

Charlene lived for a few years after this. Her discarnate Helpers had promised to be with her whenever she had need. This time they did not help her to remain in her body; instead they assisted her to leave it easily.

Twice in the months following her death she came to meet with us, her friends, as we were working together with one of us in hypnosis. She didn't wait to be called but came voluntarily, and when we asked about another friend, also a nurse, who had preceded her in death, she said, "She's working with the souls in Kosovo."

Occasionally a person seems to be aware not only on the higher level but almost on the conscious level that the Right Time is approaching. This apparently was the case with an eleven-year-old girl who wrote a poem that she showed to a classmate. Four days later the young poetess was struck by a car and killed. The classmate took her friend's poem to her music teacher, asking him to make a song of it.

This is the poem. Remember that although her body dies in four days, she herself will love us "Forever and ever and ever."

FOR ALL
by Carly Dann, aged eleven
(used by permission of mother)

For all the hands that I've never held,
For all the lips that I've never kissed,
For all the smiles that I've never seen shining on me,
   I love you, I always will,
   Till the day that I die
      I love you forever.

For all the eyes that I've never looked into,
For all the cheeks never felt on my face,
For all the people that I've never loved, Baby,
   I love you, I always will,
   Till the day that I die
      I love you forever.

I love you forever and ever and ever,
As long as I live I will never forget you.
For all the hands that I've never held, Baby,
   I love you . . .
      Forever.

And now as I come to the end of this book I think of the benediction ending many Eastern writings:

"PEACE TO ALL BEINGS"
—whether alive or "dead,"
whether human or non-human:
PEACE.

Epilogue

A MUSICAL COMPOSITION may end with a delicate-looking double-bar and the Italian words, *Da Capo al Fine:* "Go back to the beginning and play until you come to the word *Fine,*" "Finish." So you return to the beginning and start playing, and eventually you come to a substantial-looking double-bar, and there is the word, *Fine* (fee-nay), the End. And you stop playing. That's the end.

One famous composer figured out how to keep his music immortal, going on and on forever. At the *Da Capo* place in one of his delightful little Etudes he wrote, *Da Capo ad Infinitum:* "Back to the beginning, play to here, and go back again to the beginning, play to here, and so on to infinity!" Smart fellow. His piece might appear to have an ending, but no: *"Da Capo ad infinitum"*!

And no heavy double-bar at all. No real Finish, no End.

Friends, that is the way our individual music is composed and marked. Each lifetime, each "piece" of music, has its own personality, its own expression of an individuality, and then it comes to a place where there seems to be an ending. There is a double-bar cutting cross the staff of lines on which our music is written (our culture, family, social, educational, and financial structure). We may think that double-bar is really terminal.

However, we notice after the music has ceased that there are words of instruction there; perhaps we did not notice them before the music came to a stop. They tell us, "Go back to a Beginning, and play again."

Following instructions, we do so. This time the music, derived from the former piece, is more varied and interesting, more developed, although following a similar basic Theme. When we arrive at that seemingly terminal point again, we softly slow the music into silence, pause, and then with more confidence return again—to another Beginning and a new variation of our Theme, still more mature and beautiful than before.

If we have become petulant, like children forced to practice when they do not wish to, and we bang out angry chords for a while, those chords may spoil the beauty temporarily but only for a while. Then, perhaps penitently or perhaps after a period of sulking, we begin our practicing again, this time with more care and patience. We are learning and maturing in wisdom and in beauty. So we come once more to an ending—the one with the delicate double-bar—the temporary ending.

There is no heavy double-bar. There is no *Fine.* No End. Our Themes direct the character of our music each time around. Hate pushes people together time after time until they cease banging harsh chords at each other. Love draws people together time after time, as long as they "make beautiful music together." Even if occasionally they drop in a sour note, or even if they insert a dissonant minor interlude or a wild cadenza or a somber coda, the basic loveliness of their Themes reappears, lifetime after lifetime.

So, friends, pass the word! There is always more music.

GLOSSARY

Absolute, The: God; the Source; the SELF: the First Creator.

Akashic Records: the permanent record of all events; the Memory of Nature, discernible by psychics or persons in hypnosis.

Astral body: the body in which one finds himself after death; the organized emotions and desires; the bio-electric aura.

Astral Plane, Astral Level: the invisible field of emotional and desire life; the next stage after death of the body.

Aura: the egg-shaped body of bio-electric energy and astral substance (emotional and feeling) that surrounds and interpenetrates a physical body; visible to clairvoyants as a shell of colored lights around living beings.

Blended Consciousness: the two-layered awareness of a person in hypnotic regression who is in contact with both past and present at the same time.

Carpenter of Galilee: Jesus of Nazareth.

Causal Level: the Abstract (upper) Mental Level, at which after death the experiences of the lives are condensed into traits and propensities, talents and Predispositions.

Cheyne-Stokes breathing: deep breathing alternating with periods of rapid shallow breathing or cessation of breathing.

Cognitive Mind, Conscious Mind: the reasoning part of the mind, active during waking awareness; also present in hypnosis to a greater or lesser degree during regressions.

Consciousness, parallel or split: may be same as Blended Consciousness.

Dark entities: disembodied entities/energies associated with negative or evil influences and activities.

Darkness: the psychospiritual realm of ignorance and evil.

Earth-bound: trapped in an intermediate state between the physical and the astral, an undesirable condition that may be due to any of numerous causes.

Evolvement: unfoldment, evolution, spiritual growth.

Galilee, Carpenter of: Jesus of Nazareth.

Gautama: family name of the young sage who became the Buddha.

Guides: discarnate helpers and assistants of humanity, still evolving themselves.

Heavens: states of happiness and bliss above the astral planes.

Hell: state of misery and frustration self-created by a soul that has caused misery to others. No eternal fiery torment.

Higher Levels: invisible realms above the Middle Astral, especially the Mental Levels (also those still higher). Contacted in meditation or hypnosis.

Higher Mind, Higher Self: the superconsciousness of an individual, wise and powerful; the Inner Self Helper; the divine Spark; "that of God within."

Ideomotor movements: muscular movements, e.g., finger movements, produced by subconscious knowledge in answer to questions answerable by Yes or No.

Interlife: the period between earth-incarnations during which the soul is actively learning and assimilating its previous earth-life experiences.

Judging, Judgment: a stage soon after death of the body in which each soul sees its life and actions, judges each thought and deed itself, and comes to conclusions about its spiritual state.

Karma: the spiritual law of Compensation, the Law of Justice, which works from causes to effects through lifetimes: "What you sow is what you will reap."

Light: universal symbol of good, of unselfishness and love. **The Light**: brilliant white light seen during or after death, felt by the one perceiving it to be a Being of light—living, intelligent, all-forgiving, loving: God.

Master: a human or discarnate soul of advanced spiritual wisdom, saintliness, and power, assisting embodied humanity from mental levels by offering thoughts and suggesting decisions. Never invading nor coercing those whom they seek to help.

Memory Bank: memory of the totality of a person's experiences, including thoughts and words, saved in the subconscious and superconscious parts of the mind of each individual.

Memory of Nature: same as the Akashic Records. Also called The Book of Life. Permanent record of everything that has occurred or been thought in the Universe; perceived by clairvoyants in various symbolic ways or as regressions.

Mental Body: the aura of bio-electric energy associated with a person's mentality; the "body" of the mind made of mental "substance." It interpenetrates and extends out beyond the astral body. Seen by clairvoyants.

NDE, Near-Death Experience: out-of-body experience occurring to an individual in a life-threatening situation or during a period of cessation of life-processes (death); reported by the individual later, after return to life.

Obsessing entities: human or non-human entities which have invaded a living person. Not multiple personalities, though causing similar confusion in the host. Each has its own life history and death-experience. Contacted in hypnosis.

Obsession: the invasion of a person by a human or non-human entity which parasitizes but does not entirely displace the resident consciousness; not complete possession.

Paradise: a state or plane of happiness after death, lower than the heavens; Upper Astral states; Elysian Fields.

Paul: the Apostle; Pharisee who turned from persecuting Christians to becoming a chief bearer of early Christian teachings to the Gentiles. Author of the Epistles of Paul.

Planning Stage: stage in the "descent" of a soul into re-incarnation preceding actual entry into embryo or fetus during which counselors assist soul in choosing main events of coming earth-life.

Psychic: a person endowed with extrasensory talents such as clairvoyance, clairaudience, telepathy, etc. Also an adjective describing these talents.

Rebirth: the birth into physical incarnation of a soul which has already lived and died before.

Reincarnation: literally, "again into flesh"; same as rebirth.

Releasement: the release by hypnosis (or other means) of obsessing entities from an obsessed person, and the simultaneous release of the person from the entities and the release of both from negative emotions and memories.

Rescue Work: the discovery of wandering souls, ghosts, etc., and helping them to leave the earth-bound condition and progress into the Light, to an appropriate level.

Review Stage: the stage soon after death in which the soul sees its previous life unroll in all its aspects, both important and trivial, both negative and positive.

Soul: the living, invisible element of an individual which wears the physical body as an outer garment, the personality as an inner garment, and remains conscious and evolving after death.

Spirit: the eternal divine spark of livingness from the Source of all life which wears the soul as its garment; the divine spark in every creature; the Higher Self, part of the SELF.

Subconscious Mind: the not-conscious part of the mind which contains the memories of everything connected to the individual through all its lives. It seeks the good of the person but does not reason nor evaluate logically. Therefore it is the source of compulsions, phobias, panics, etc.

Superconscious Mind: the not-conscious part of the mind which remains wise, steady, firm, incorruptible and is in contact with all other superconscious minds, sharing knowledge with them while still retaining intimate connection with the individual; the Higher Mind; the Inner Self Helper. Can be considered synonymous with the Spirit.

Superconscious Level: in hypnosis or meditation, that condition or state in which the Higher Mind is accessed and addressed and in which the wisdom of the Higher Self is received.

Teachers: human or discarnate beings more evolved than Guides, who remain close to embodied humanity to offer instruction and help when requested. Like Guides and Masters, they do not invade nor compel but are respectful of one's free will. Will become Masters on further spiritual development.

Universal Mind: the Subconscious Mind of the Universe; the Framework of the Universe, "which responds to demands but does not command"; the sum total of Natural Laws that govern the processes of physical, psychological and spiritual beings and events.

BIBLIOGRAPHY

Bailey, Alice A. & Djwhal Khul (1983). *Death: The Great Adventure*. Compilation from earlier books. Lucis Pub. Co., New York, NY.

Baldwin, William J., DDS, Ph.D. (1992). *Spirit Releasement Therapy: A Technique Manual*, 2nd edition. Headline Books, Inc., Tera Alta, WV.

Banks, Hal N., S.T.D. (1987). *Death: A Preface (A Continuing Journey)*, Maverick Publications, Bend, OR.

Warren, Henry C. (1896). *Buddhism in Translations*, Harvard Oriental Series, Vol. III, Harvard University Press, Cambridge, MA.

Chaplin, Annabel (1977). *The Bright Light of Death*, DeVorss and Company, Marina del Rey, CA.

Dowding, Lord Hugh (1945). *Lychgate: The Entrance to the Path*, Rider and Company, London, England.

Eadie, Betty J. (1992). *Embraced by the Light*, Bantam Books/Gold Leaf Press, Placerville, CA.

Fiore, Edith, Ph.D. (1987). *The Unquiet Dead*, Doubleday and Company, Inc., Garden City, NY.

Gershom, Rabbi Yonassan (1992). *Beyond the Ashes*, A.R.E. Press, Virginia Beach, VA.

Hampton, Charles (1943). *The Transition Called Death*, The Theosophical Publishing House, Wheaton, IL.

Heindel, Max (1929). *The Rosicrucian Cosmoconception*, L.N. Fowler and Company, Ludgate Circus, London.

Hickman, Irene, D.O. (1994). *Remote Depossession*, Hickman Systems, Kirksville, MO.

Ireland-Frey, Louise (1986). "Clinical Depossession: Releasement of Attached Entities from Unsuspecting Hosts," *Journal of Regression Therapy, Vol. 1*, No. 2, pp. 90-101.

Ireland-Frey, Louise (1999). *Freeing the Captives: The Emerging Therapy of Treating Spirit Attachment*, Hampton Roads Publishing Co., Charlottesville, VA.

Keyes, Ken., Jr. (1982). *The Hundredth Monkey*, Vision Books, Coos Bay, OR.

Kübler-Ross, Elizabeth (1991). *On Life After Death*, Celestial Arts, Berkeley, CA.

Loehr, Franklin (1986). *Diary After Death* (fiction), Religious Research Press, Grand Island, FL.

Long, Max Freedom (1948, 1976). *The Secret Science Behind Miracles*, DeVorss and Company, Marina del Rey, CA.

Lucas, Winafred B., Ph.D. (1993). *Regression Therapy: A Handbook for Professionals*, Deep Forest Press, Crest Park, CA.

Maurey, Eugene (1988). *Exorcism*, Whitford Press, West Chester, PA.

Meek, George W. (1980). *After We Die, What Then?*, Metascience Corporation, Franklin, NC.

Monroe, Robert A. (1985). *Far Journeys*, Doubleday and Company, Inc., Garden City, NY.

Moody, Raymond A., Jr., M.D. (1975). *Life After Life*, Bantam/Mockingbird Books, New York, NY.

Naegeli-Osjord, M.D. (1988). *Possession and Exorcism*, New Frontiers Center, OR, WI.

Netherton, Morris, Ph.D. & Nancy Shiffrin (1978). *Past Lives Therapy*, William Morrow and Company, Inc., New York, NY.

Rawlings, Maurice, M.D. (1978). *Beyond Death's Door*, Thomas Nelson/Bantam, New York, NY.

Ritchie, George C., M.D. & Elizabeth Sherrill (1978). *Return from Tomorrow*, Fleming H. Revell Company, Old Tappan, NJ.

Sutphen, Dick (1978). *Past Lives, Future Loves*. Pocket Books/Simon and Schuster, New York, NY.

Tompkins, Peter & Christopher Bird (1973). *The Secret Life of Plants*, Harper and Row, New York, NY.

Weatherhead, Leslie D. (1969). *LIFE Begins at Death*, Abingdon Press, Nashville, TN.

Whitton, Joel J., M.D., Ph.D. & Joe Fisher (1986). *Life Between Life*, Warner/Doubleday, New York, NY.

Wickland, Carl A., M.D. (1924; Newcastle ed., 1974). *Thirty Years Among the Dead*, Newcastle Publishing Company. Inc., Van Nuys, CA.

ABOUT THE AUTHOR

LOUISE IRELAND-FREY, M.D., had her first encounter with death in Colorado as a young girl, when she had several flashbacks to a past life when she drowned in the ocean—as a boy in China. Interest in such subjects continued through college (at CU Boulder), graduate school (at Mt. Holyoke College, Massachusetts), and medical school (at Tulane University). While in medical school she received membership in Alpha Omega Alpha, the Honor Medical Society, and graduated in 1940 near the top of her class.

In 1979, after conquering a health problem of many years through self-hypnosis, she took more training and became a hypnotherapist. Past-life encounters were frequent among her clients, and, as she reminds us, "When one has lived before, one has died before." She states unequivocally, "Consciousness does continue after the body dies."

Dr. Ireland-Frey is retired and lives in Durango, Colorado. In her late 80s, she is rounding up her life in anticipation of the next major step, her Transition.

Printed in the United States
21740LVS00002B/256-258

9 781577 330905